Governance of Budgeting

Some Guiding Principles

Governance of Budgeting

Some Guiding Principles

By

H.S. Nath

CYBER TECH PUBLICATIONS

4264/3, Ansari Road, Daryaganj, New Delhi-110002

Ph.: 011-23244078, 011-43559448 Fax: 011-23280028

E-Mail: cyberpublicationsdelhi@yahoo.com

E.mail: cybertechpublications@g.mail.com

website: www.cybertechpublications.com

GOVERNANCE OF BUDGETING
Some Guiding Principles

H.S.NATH

First Edition 2011

Asian Offset Printers

Published by
G.S. Rawat for Cyber Tech Publications
4264/3, Ansari Road, Daryaganj, New Delhi-110002 (India)
Ph.: 011-23244078, 011-43559448 Fax: 011-23280028
E-Mail: cyberpublicationsdelhi@yahoo.com
cyberpublications@gmail.com
Website: www.cybertechpublications.com

Contents

Preface

> "The trouble with the average budget is that it's hard to fill up one hole without digging another."
>
> —*Dan Bennet*

Budgeting is the process of determining and recording the expected financial provision for a future period, generally the next financial year. Budget preparation is a great work involving skill of financial wizards. Budget day is the great occasion in the economic life of a country. Since dynamics of development of a nation and its economy heavily rests upon the quality of national budget, every care is taken to make it progressive so that it may serve the purpose one and all concerned.

Budget and budgeting are the key issues of interest to many economists, financial wizards and economic analysts. As such wider debates are held on and comments of experts are elicited and soughts thereupon.

The present work is modest attempt at elucidating all salient features and prime issues of the governance of budgeting. All allied features are also given an elaborate treatment. The following chapters make core of the study: Budget and Budgeting: An Overview; What is Finance?; Fundamentals of Budget Preparation; Public Finance and Public Budgeting; Budgeting and Accounting in India;

Budget in Parliament; Union Budget of India 2010; Government Debt and Allied Issues; Taxation in Budgeting and Deficit Budgeting etc. followed by Glossary, Appendices and Bibliography.

Certainly, the contents will enlighten and delight one and all concerned.

With the sole aim of furnishing authoritative information, we have corroborated the findings and expert views of many scholars of repute in the field. We express our gratitude to them all and the sources of information. My colleagues and friends have helped me a lot in conceputalising the outline of this work. I am grateful to them also. Finally, I am thankful to my publishers for materializing this book elegantly in the present shape.

Comments and constructive criticism are welcome from all quarters to enhance the utility and quality of information contained herein.

—H.S. Nath

1

Budget and Budgeting: An Overview

> A "budget" is a *plan* for the accomplishment of *programs* related to *objectives* and *goals* within a definite *time* period, including an estimate of *resources required*, together with an estimate of *resources available*, usually compared with one or more *past periods* and *showing future requirements*.
>
> —*Smith and Lynch*

A budget, originally derived from old French *bougette*, meaning purse, is generally a list of all planned expenses and revenues. It is a plan for saving and spending. A budget is an important concept in microeconomics, which uses a budget line to illustrate the trade-offs between two or more goods. In other terms, a budget is an organizational plan stated in monetary terms.

The purpose of budgeting is can be summarised as follows:

1. Provide a forecast of revenues and expenditures i.e. construct a model of how our business might perform financially speaking if certain strategies, events and plans are carried out.
2. Enable the actual financial operation of the business to be measured against the forecast.

The process of calculating the costs of starting a small business begins with a list of all necessary purchases including tangible assets (for example, equipment, inventory) and services (for example, remodeling, insurance), working capital, sources and collateral. The budget should contain a narrative explaining how you decided on the amount of this reserve and a description of the expected financial results of business activities. The assets should be valued with each and every cost. All other expenses are like labour factory overhead all freshmen expenses are also included into business budgeting

Corporate Budget

The budget of a company is often compiled annually, but may not be. A finished budget, usually requiring considerable effort, is a plan for the short-term future, typically one year (*see Budget Year*). While traditionally the Finance department compiles the company's budget, modern software allows hundreds or even thousands of people in various departments (operations, human resources, IT etc) to list their expected revenues and expenses in the final budget.

If the actual figures delivered through the budget period come close to the budget, this suggests that the managers understand their business and have been successfully driving it in the intended direction. On the other hand, if the figures diverge wildly from the budget, this sends an 'out of control' signal, and the share price could suffer as a result.

Event Management Budget

A budget is a fundamental tool for an event director to predict with reasonable accuracy whether the event will result in a profit, a loss or will break-even. A budget can also be used as a pricing tool.

Government Budget

A government budget is a legal document that is often passed by the legislature, and approved by the chief executive-or president. For example, only certain types of revenue may be imposed and collected. Property tax is frequently the basis for municipal and county revenues, while sales tax and/or income tax are the basis for state revenues, and income tax and corporate tax are the basis for national revenues.

The two basic elements of any budget are the revenues and expenses. In the case of the government, revenues are derived primarily from taxes. Government expenses include spending on current goods and services, which economists call government consumption; government investment expenditures such as infrastructure investment or research expenditure; and transfer payments like unemployment or retirement benefits.

Budgets have an economic, political and technical basis. Unlike a pure economic budget, they are not entirely designed to allocate scarce resources for the best economic use. They also have a political basis wherein different interests push and pull in an attempt to obtain benefits and avoid burdens. The technical element is the forecast of the likely levels of revenues and expenses.

The budget of a government is a summary or plan of the intended revenues and expenditures of that government.

The United States federal budget is prepared by the Office of Management and Budget, and submitted to Congress for consideration. Invariably, Congress makes many and substantial changes. Nearly all American states are required to have balanced budgets, but the federal government is allowed to run deficits.

The UK Budget is prepared by the Treasury under the direction of the Chancellor of the Exchequer. Parliament rarely makes any significant amendments.

Personal or Family Budget

In a personal or family budget all sources of income (inflows) are identified and expenses (outflows) are planned with the intent of matching outflows to inflows (making ends meet.) In consumer theory, the equation restricting an individual or household to spend no more than its total resources is often called the budget constraint.

Budget Types

Sales budget: The sales budget is an estimate of future sales, often broken down into both units and dollars. It is used to create company sales goals.

Production budget: Product oriented companies create a production budget which estimates the number of units that must be manufactured to meet the sales goals. The production budget also estimates the various costs involved with manufacturing those units, including labor and material.

Cash Flow/Cash budget: The cash flow budget is a prediction of future cash receipts and expenditures for a particular time period. It usually covers a period in the short term future. The cash flow budget helps the business determine when income will be sufficient to cover expenses and when the company will need to seek outside financing.

Marketing budget: The marketing budget is an

estimate of the funds needed for promotion, advertising, and public relations in order to market the product or service.

Project budget: The project budget is a prediction of the costs associated with a particular company project. These costs include labor, materials, and other related expenses. The project budget is often broken down into specific tasks, with task budgets assigned to each.

Revenue budget: The Revenue Budget consists of revenue receipts of government and the expenditure met from these revenues. Tax revenues are made up of taxes and other duties that the government levies.

Expenditure budget: A budget type which include of spending data items.

BALANCED BUDGET

A balanced budget is when there is neither a budget deficit or a budget surplus – when revenues equal expenditure ("the accounts *balance*") – particularly by a government. More generally, it refers to when there is no deficit, but possibly a surplus. A *cyclically* balanced budget is a budget that is not necessarily balanced year-to-year, but is balanced over the economic cycle, running a surplus in boom years and running a deficit in lean years, with these offsetting over time. Balanced budgets, and the associated topic of budget deficits, are a contentious point within academic economics and within politics, notably American politics. The mainstream economic view is that having a balanced budget in every year is not desirable, with budget deficits is lean times being desirable. Within American politics the situation is much more debated, with all US states other than Vermont having a balanced budget amendment of some form, while conversely the US federal government has generally run a deficit since the late 1960s, and the topic of balanced budgets being a consistent topic of debate. In rare cases large budget *surpluses* may also be banned, as in the Oregon kicker.

Mainstream economics mainly advocates a cyclically balanced budget, arguing from the perspective Keynesian economics that budget deficits provide fiscal stimulus in lean times, while budget surpluses provide restraint in boom times. Alternative currents in the mainstream and branches of heterodox economics argue differently, with some arguing that budget deficits are always harmful, and others arguing that budget deficits are both beneficial and in fact *necessary.*

Schools categorically opposed to budget deficits include the freshwater school of mainstream economics and neoclassical economics more generally, and the Austrian school of economics. Budget deficits are argued to be necessary by some within Post-Keynesian economics, notably the Chartalist school.

> *Larger deficits,* sufficient to recycle savings out of a growing gross domestic product (GDP) in excess of what can be recycled by profit-seeking private investment, are not an economic sin but *an economic necessity.*

In the United States, the fiscal conservatism movement believes that balanced budgets are an important goal. Every state other than Vermont has a balanced budget amendment, providing some form of ban on deficits, while the Oregon kicker bans *surpluses* of greater than 2% of revenue.

Balanced Budget Multiplier

Because of the multiplier effect, it is possible to change aggregate demand (Y) keeping a balanced budget. The Government increases its expenditures (G), balancing it by an increase in taxes (T). Since only part of the money taken away from households would have actually been used in the economy, the change in consumption expenditure will be smaller than the change in taxes. Therefore the money which would have been saved by households is instead injected into the economy, itself becoming part of the multiplier process. In general, a change in the balanced budget will change aggregate demand by an amount equal to the change in spending.

$$Y_1 = c_0 + c_1(Y - T) + I + G$$

$$Y_1 = \frac{1}{1 - c_1}(c_0 + I + G - c_1 T)$$

$$G = G + a$$

$$T = T + a$$

$$Y_2 = \frac{1}{1 - c_1}(c_0 + I + (G + a) - c_1(T + a))$$

$$\Delta Y = Y_2 - Y_1 = \frac{a}{1 - c_1}(1 - c_1) = a$$

$$\Delta T - \Delta G = a - a = 0$$

BUDGET DAY

Budget Day is the day that a government presents its Budget to a legislature for approval, typically in a ceremonial fashion. It only exists in some countries of the world. In particular, the United States does not have a Budget Day. There, the legislation that establishes the federal government's budget originates in the Congress, although the executive branch traditionally makes a proposal in advance, often amid some ceremony.

In India and other erstwhile colonies of British Empire, Budgeting is done on British lines. Here in this section we give an account of this ceremony.

In Ireland, Budget Day is the annual statement to the Dáil by the Minister for Finance, made in the first week of December. It sets out the budgetary targets for the following year and consists of (i) a Financial Statement to the Dáil, (ii) Budgetary Measures (a list of budgetary changes detailing the cost/yield of same), (iii) Budget Statistics and Tables and (iv) various financial resolutions.

The day itself is very similar to Budget Day in the United Kingdom. In the early afternoon, the Minister for Finance will normally hold a photocall in the car park of Leinster House, with the traditional *budget briefcase* (in recent years, a floppy disk or CD-ROM purportely containing the contents of the Budget speech has often been used instead). At 15:45, the Minister for Finance presents the budget speech in Dáil Éireann. The speech, which lasts approximetly one hour, is normally carried live on Raidió Teilifís Éireann radio and television. The speech contains the main taxation and other fiscal measures to be employed over the next calendar year. The Opposition Front Bench spokesperson on Finance normally replies to the Budget speech first, followed by the spokespersons on finance of other opposition parties. A vote on supply normally takes place before midnight on the night of the budget, with changes to excise duties on alcohol, tobacco, and petrol taking place from midnight. Most other measures are spelt out in greater detail in the Finance Bill which is introduced in the Oireachtas following the budget, eventually becoming the Finance Act.

In the United Kingdom, Budget Day is the day that the Chancellor of the Exchequer delivers the Budget, first privately to the Budget Cabinet and then publicly in a speech to the House of Commons. It is always aligned with the fiscal year, which itself in the UK is still aligned with the Julian Calendar. Nowadays, Budget Day occurs on a Wednesday in March, before the start of the new fiscal year, although in the early 20th century it was delivered in April, after the start of the fiscal year.

Chancellors have had varying opinions on Budget Day. Nigel Lawson wrote, in his memoirs, that it is "best described as an enjoyable ordeal". Harold Macmillan, in explaining his surprise at being appointed Chancellor, said that he thought Budget Day to be "rather like a school Speech Day: a bit of a bore, but there it is".

Preparation

The Chancellor, Treasury ministers, and officials will have been working on the Budget some time in advance of Budget Day. Geoffrey Howe initiated the tradition of a weekend meeting, for all Treasury ministers and officials, outside of London and some time in advance of Budget Day, for discussing the Budget. This meeting is now a customary part of the annual Budget preparations.

Presentation to the Monarch

The monarch is the first person to be told of the Budget. Queen Elizabeth II has customarily invited the Chancellor to dinner the day before Budget Day, where she is given an outline of the Budget.

Presentation to the Cabinet

The Budget is presented to the Cabinet before being presented to Parliament. Formally, the Cabinet has power to amend the Budget. In practice, however, this is made impossible by the fact that the Budget Cabinet meets on the very morning of Budget Day itself, far too late for any but very minor changes to be effected.

The Budget is presented to the Cabinet largely as a *fait accompli* by the Chancellor, the various junior Treasury ministers, and the Prime Minister (in the rôle of the First Lord of the Treasury).

This swiftness is justified on the grounds of secrecy. It is considered essential the budget details not leak before the Chancellor's public speech. (In 1936, James Henry Thomas famously leaked Budget details after the Budget Cabinet, which at the time was being held five days before Budget Day, which had been until that point the traditional period between the Budget Cabinet and Budget Day itself.) Little objection has apparently been raised by the Cabinet to this. The only times that the Budget Cabinet has raised objections causing last-minute amendment to the Budget have been:

1945

Hugh Dalton removed a proposal to change the tax on fuel oil.

1951

Hugh Gaitskell responded to Cabinet pressure and abandoned his plans for a differential fuel tax.

1962

Cabinet persuaded Selwyn Lloyd to announce the early abolition of the tax on home owner-occupiers.

1981

The so-called "wets" in the Cabinet persuaded Geoffrey Howe to increase the state pension in line with inflation, which he had not wanted to do. (Margaret Thatcher recorded in her memoirs that "[t]he dissenters in the Cabinet ... had been stunned by the budget when they learnt its contents".)

The Chancellor's Speech and Debate

The Chancellor's Speech in the House is given immediately after what is usually a somewhat lacklustre Prime Minister's Question Time, it being largely overshadowed by what is seen as the main Parliamentary event of the day, now usually around 12:30 but previously about 15:30. Nigel Lawson reports that after the press photo-call at 15:15, where like all chancellors he would hold the red dispatch box, purportedly containing the budget speech, aloft; he used to spend time in his room, just behind the Speaker's chair, collecting his thoughts, before entering the house at 15:25, usually to the sound of "a roar from the Government benches".

It has varied in length over the years. Macmillan remarked that he "would try not to prolong the agony", and once opined of the speech that he did not think it "necessary to start with the usual long review of the events of the last financial year". It is also a parliamentary tradition that whilst making the Budget Speech the Chancellor may drink whatever they wish including alcohol, which is otherwise forbidden. Past Chancellors have opted for: whisky (Kenneth Clarke), gin and tonic (Geoffrey Howe), brandy and water (Benjamin Disraeli), spritzer (Nigel Lawson) and sherry and beaten egg (William Ewart Gladstone). Alistair Darling, opted for water like his predecessor Gordon Brown.

The Speech is followed by a debate, which can last for several days. In theory, the report and the financial proposals that the Chancellor sets out in the speech are immediately considered and debated by the House, with the Chancellor in attendance to respond to arguments and, occasionally, to amend proposals. Young reports one Member of Parliament observing that Chancellors customarily "keep up their sleeves one or two million pounds which they propose to give away in concessions during the course of the Finance Bill debates".

In practice, practical concerns dictate otherwise. Nigel Lawson reports that "[as] soon as MPs realize that the tax announcements are over they dash out of the Chamber to get their copies of the *Financial Statement and Budget Report* — the 'Red Book'".

Similarly, there is a rush by the news services to report Budget items. Young observed in the 1960s that newspapers were "on the street, within minutes it seemed, bringing the glad tidings: TUPPENCE OFF BEER. INCOME TAX DOWN.". Since the televisation of Parliament, television news services have broadcast the Chancellor's speech live, as a "Budget special".

In the Evening

Since 1952, the Chancellor has, in the evening of Budget Day, made a television party political broadcast about the budget. Similar broadcasts are made, in response, by representatives of the major Opposition parties. All broadcasts are arranged through the normal Parliamentary processes for arranging party election broadcasts.

Aftermath

The Finance Bill proper is only itself presented to Parliament some time after Budget Day, and is debated for days or even weeks afterwards. It is common for the bill to be passed, becoming the Finance Act, some time in late July. The Act back-dates its provisions, so that they take effect from either from Budget Day itself, or from the start of the fiscal year.

STAGES IN BUDGET PROCESS (INDIA)

STAGE 1: Estimates. Part A - Expenditure: The Indian Constitution requires the government to present to Parliament a statement that shows separately the expected revenues and expenditures, both current and capital by heads of account.

The Budget-making process, in normal times, gets set in motion by the third quarter of the financial year.

On the expenditure side, initial estimates are provided by the various ministries. There are two components of expenditure - plan and non-plan. Of these, plan expenditures are estimated after discussions between each of the ministries concerned and the Planning Commission.

Apart from allocations for continuing plan programmes initiated in earlier fiscal year, the Planning Commission decides on the new programmes that can be undertaken on the basis of a tentative estimate or resources available for plan expenditure that is provided to it by the finance ministry.

Non-plain expenditure for various ministries are prepared by their financial advisors. These are sent to the expenditure secretary who, after exhaustive discussions with financial advisors, makes an assessment of the likely expenditures for the ensuing fiscal year.

In one sense, the assessment of likely non-plan

expenditure is comparatively simple. Nearly 90 per cent of the non-plan expenditure is accounted for by interest payments, subsidies (mainly on food and fertilisers) and wage payments to employees.

STAGE 1: Estimates. Part B - Revenue: Parallel to the exercises on the expenditure side, an assessment is made of the revenues which are likely to flow into the government kitty. Revenue receipts, like expenditure, are of two types - capital and current receipts.

Capital receipts include repayment of loans made by the federal government, receipts from divestment of public-sector equity and borrowings - both domestic and external.

Current receipts, by and large, include tax revenues, receipts by way of dividends from public-sector units and interest payments on loans given out by the federal government.

While both dividends from public-sector units and interest receipts are fairly easy to assess, the amounts received by way of tax revenues is estimated on the basis of existing rates of taxation and an assessment of the likely growth and inflation rate over the ensuing fiscal year.

On the capital receipts side, targeted amounts to be realised through divestment of public sector equity and amounts to be realised by way of repayments of loans is made. All the estimates flow to the revenue secretary.

STAGE 2: First estimates of deficit: Once this exercise is completed expenditure estimates are matched with revenue estimate to arrive at a first estimate of the shortfall in revenue to meet projected expenditure.

Following this the government, in tandem with its

chief economic advisor, determines the optimum level of borrowings that the government can resort to.

The level of external borrowings is an easily estimated figure because much of the external borrowing on government account consists of bilateral and multilateral assistance which is known by the time budget exercises are undertaken.

The level of domestic borrowing depends partly on the desired level of fiscal deficit that the government targets for itself. A part of the revenue gap is left unfilled to be met through the issue of ad hoc treasury bills. Over the past few years, this gap, called the overall budget deficit, is government by an understanding between the Reserve Bank of India [Get Quote] and the finance ministry on the maximum level of ad hoc treasury bills that can be issued during a fiscal year.

This has been done to ensure that the issue of ad hoc treasury bills to fill revenue gaps does not lead to problems of monetary management.

STAGE 3: Narrowing of the deficit: After the targets for the fiscal deficits and the overall budget deficit have been decided by the government, any remaining shortfall is filled through a revision in tax rates where considered feasible and in keeping with fiscal incentive structure the government wishes to put in place to stimulate the growth in different sectors.

Subsequently adjustments are made in expenditures, should it be required, to ensure that the fiscal and overall deficit remain at targeted levels.

Such adjustments in expenditure are usually made on the plan side - the only item of expenditure that offers any scope for adjustments. With nearly 90 per cent of non-plan expenditure being accounted for by interest payments, subsidies and administrative expenditure and the political sensitivities involved in reducing subsidies, non-plan expenditure of the Indian government is characterised by an extraordinary degree of rigidity.

Inevitably, therefore, plan expenditures are determined as a residual after pre-emptions have already been made for non-plan expenditure.

STAGE 4: The Budget: The presentation of the Budget for the ensuing fiscal year (beginning April 1) is usually done on the last working day of February. Parliamentary scrutiny of proposals and the passage of the budget does not normally get completed until the second week of May, well after the commencement of the new fiscal year.

Since expenditures cannot be incurred in a new fiscal year without Parliamentary approval, the government usually seeks an interim approval to meet emergent expenditures that have to be incurred pending the approval of the budget.

This is called the vote-on-account and the sanctions given by the passage of the vote-on-account get automatically overridden once the Budget is approved by Parliament.

COUNTRYWISE GOVERNMENT BUDGET

This article includes a chart representing revenues, expenditures and resulting deficit or surplus of government budget. The countries are ranked by budget revenues. The data is taken mainly from CIA World Factbook.

Due to political reasons (unusually high expenses of the USA central government), for the USA only federal budget is shown (it is approximately a half of total governmental budgets in the country). Almost for all other countries the total budget is shown. Weight of central government budgets in federal countries is usually much smaller fraction (for instance, ~ 20-25% in Germany) in total governmental budget and <10% of GDP. It should also be noted that in some federations such a Mexico only the Federal budget it shown and the total does not include the budgets of state governments which collect between 35%-75% of all tax income, meaning that for some nations the total government budget may be substatially higher if the state government budgets were included in the total.

Rank	*Country*	*Revenues (million $)*	*Expenditures (million $)*	*Deficit/surplus (million $)*	*Date*
1	United States (Federal Budget only)	1,914,000.0	3,615,000.0	-1,701,000.0	2009 est.
2	Japan	1,614,000.0	1,997,000.0	-383,000.0	2009 est.
3	Germany	1,398,000.0	1,540,000.0	-142,000.0	2009 est.
4	France	1,229,000.0	1,445,000.0	-216,000.0	2009 est.
5	China	972,300.0	1,137,000.0	-164,700.0	2009 est.
6	Italy	960,100.0	1,068,000.0	-107,900.0	2009 est.
7	United Kingdom	819,900.0	1,132,000.0	-312,100.0	2009 est.
8	Brazil	657,900.0	657,900.0	+0.0	2009 est.
9	Canada	514,500.0	547,200.0	-32,700.0	2009 est.
10	Spain	420,400.0	536,300.0	-115,900.0	2009 est.
11	Netherlands	408,500.0	398,800.0	+9,700.0	2008 est.
12	Russia	383,500.0	273,500.0	+110,000.0	2008 est.
13	Australia	343,600.0	340,700.0	+2,900.0	2008 est.
14	Saudi Arabia	293,000.0	136,000.0	+157,000.0	2008 est.
15	Norway	283,700.0	197,000.0	+86,700.0	2008 est.
16	Sweden	270,500.0	258,600.0	+11,900.0	2008 est.
17	Mexico	256,700.0	256,800.0	-100.0	2008 est.
18	Belgium	251,300.0	254,200.0	-2,900.0	2008 est.
19	South Korea	232,200.0	222,900.0	+9,300.0	2008 est.
20	Austria	198,600.0	203,000.0	-4,400.0	2008 est.
21	Denmark	192,000.0	177,600.0	+14,400.0	2008 est.

22	Switzerland	173,600.0	168,200.0	+5,400.0	2008 est.
23	Turkey	164,600.0	176,300.0	-11,700.0	2008 est.
24	India	153,500.0	205,300.0	-51,800.0	2008 est.
25	Finland	143,800.0	132,300.0	+11,500.0	2008
26	Greece	132,400.0	143,800.0	-11,400.0	2008 est.
27	Poland	117,000.0	127,300.0	-10,300.0	2008 est.
28	Kuwait	113,300.0	63,550.0	+49,750.0	2008 est.
29	Portugal	108,600.0	114,700.0	-6,100.0	2008 est.
30	Venezuela	106,200.0	100,800.0	+5,400.0	2008 est.
31	Indonesia	101,100.0	101,600.0	-500.0	2008 est.
32	Iran	97,710.0	84,780.0	+12,930.0	FY09/10 est.
33	Czech Republic	94,960.0	99,460.0	-4,500.0	2008 est.
34	Ireland	93,840.0	110,800.0	-16,960.0	2008 est.
35	Argentina	86,300.0	80,400.0	+5,900.0	2008 est.
36	South Africa	83,850.0	83,300.0	+550.0	2008 est.
37	United Arab Emirates	83,150.0	48,300.0	+34,850.0	2008 est.
38	Colombia	76,420.0	78,490.0	-2,070.0	2008 est.
39	Hungary	76,200.0	81,500.0	-5,300.0	2008 est.
40	Algeria	73,260.0	51,190.0	+22,070.0	2008 est.
41	Israel	68,440.0	70,060.0	-1,620.0	2008 est.
42	Ukraine	65,020.0	68,480.0	-3,460.0	2008 est.
43	Romania	64,440.0	71,160.0	-6,720.0	2008 est.
44	Libya	56,350.0	29,120.0	+27,230.0	2008 est.
45	New Zealand	55,100.0	54,660.0	+440.0	2008 est.
—	Taiwan	50,910.0	54,700.0	-3,790.0	2008 est.
46	Chile	46,500.0	37,700.0	+8,800.0	2008 est.
47	Thailand	45,300.0	55,760.0	-10,460.0	2008 est.
48	Slovakia	44,860.0	46,960.0	-2,100.0	2008 est.
49	Malaysia	44,320.0	55,010.0	-10,690.0	2008 est.
50	Iraq	42,400.0	49,900.0	-7,500.0	FY08 est.
51	Cuba	41,060.0	43,330.0	-2,270.0	2008 est.
52	Egypt	40,460.0	51,380.0	-10,920.0	2008 est.
53	Qatar	40,360.0	28,080.0	+12,280.0	2008 est.
54	Peru	38,830.0	35,500.0	+3,330.0	2008 est.
—	Hong Kong	36,620.0	38,890.0	-2,270.0	2008 est.
55	Kazakhstan	29,640.0	32,600.0	-2,960.0	2008 est.
56	Nigeria	29,490.0	30,610.0	-1,120.0	2008 est.
57	Singapore	28,600.0	27,500.0	+1,100.0	2008 est.
58	Angola	27,180.0	20,600.0	+6,580.0	2008 est.

59	Philippines	26,750.0	28,200.0	-1,450.0	2008 est.
60	Morocco	26,090.0	28,410.0	-2,320.0	2008 est.
61	Belarus	25,230.0	26,050.0	-820.0	2008 est.
62	Croatia	23,710.0	23,460.0	+250.0	2008 est.
63	Slovenia	23,160.0	22,930.0	+230.0	2008 est.
64	Vietnam	22,390.0	24,190.0	-1,800.0	2008 est.
65	Luxembourg	22,250.0	22,080.0	+170.0	2008 est.
66	Pakistan	22,140.0	32,090.0	-9,950.0	2008 est.
67	Bulgaria	20,430.0	18,930.0	+1,500.0	2008
68	Ecuador	19,440.0	17,790.0	+1,650.0	2008 est.
69	Lithuania	15,400.0	15,860.0	-460.0	2008 est.
70	Oman	14,600.0	16,700.0	-2,100.0	2009 est.
71	Azerbaijan	14,510.0	15,660.0	-1,150.0	2008 est.
72	Latvia	12,330.0	12,840.0	-510.0	2008 est.
73	Sudan	11,840.0	12,950.0	-1,110.0	2008 est.
74	Cyprus	11,330.0	11,200.0	+130.0	2008 est.
75	Syria	10,900.0	13,770.0	-2,870.0	2008 est.
76	Tunisia	9,652.0	11,030.0	-1,378.0	2008 est.
77	Serbia	9,600.0	9,800.0	-200.0	2007 est.
78	Yemen	9,097.0	10,550.0	-1,453.0	2008 est.
79	Estonia	8,920.0	9,091.0	-171.0	2008 est.
80	Bangladesh	8,831.0	12,540.0	-3,709.0	2008 est.
81	Bosnia and Herzegovina	8,607.0	8,962.0	-355.0	2008 est.
82	Trinidad and Tobago	8,317.0	8,311.0	+6.0	2008 est.
83	Uruguay	8,204.0	8,526.0	-322.0	2008 est.
84	Bolivia	8,044.0	7,341.0	+703.0	2008 est.
85	Uzbekistan	8,005.0	8,127.0	-122.0	2008 est.
86	Dominican Republic	7,947.0	9,069.0	-1,122.0	2008 est.
87	Sri Lanka	7,800.0	11,000.0	-3,200.0	2009 est.
88	Iceland	7,582.0	7,159.0	+423.0	2008 est.
89	Bahrain	7,226.0	5,806.0	+1,420.0	2008 est.
90	Equatorial Guinea	7,056.0	3,779.0	+3,277.0	2008 est.
91	Lebanon	7,000.0	10,000.0	-3,000.0	2008 est.
92	Brunei	6,889.0	4,000.0	+2,889.0	2008 est.
—	Puerto Rico	6,700.0	9,600.0	-2,900.0	FY99/00
93	Kenya	6,617.0	8,196.0	-1,579.0	2008 est.
—	Macau	6,200.0	2,900.0	+3,300.0	2008
94	Panama	6,090.0	6,000.0	+90.0	2008 est.
95	Jordan	5,999.0	7,870.0	-1,871.0	2008 est.

96	Cameroon	5,371.0	4,319.0	+1,052.0	2008 est
97	Republic of the Congo	5,363.0	2,758.0	+2,605.0	2008 est.
98	Guatemala	4,944.0	5,647.0	-703.0	2008 est
99	Cote d'Ivoire	4,725.0	5,082.0	-357.0	2008 est.
100	Costa Rica	4,604.0	4,552.0	+52.0	2008 est
101	Ethiopia	4,586.0	5,729.0	-1,143.0	2008 est
102	Botswana	4,556.0	4,127.0	+429.0	2008 est
103	Gabon	4,463.0	2,746.0	+1,717.0	2008 est.
104	Tanzania	4,216.0	4,658.0	-442.0	2008 est.
105	Jamaica	4,166.0	4,838.0	-672.0	2008 est
106	Ghana	4,021.0	5,521.0	-1,500.0	2008 est.
107	El Salvador	3,928.0	4,226.0	-298.0	2008 est.
108	Georgia	3,778.0	4,182.0	-404.0	2008 est.
109	Zambia	3,777.0	4,104.0	-327.0	2008 est.
110	Albania	3,771.0	4,538.0	-767.0	2008 est.
111	Malta	3,457.0	3,653.0	-196.0	2008 est.
112	Senegal	3,141.0	3,799.0	-658.0	2008 est.
113	Papua New Guinea	3,098.0	2,949.0	+149.0	2008 est.
114	Paraguay	2,939.0	2,866.0	+73.0	2008 est.
115	Macedonia	2,889.0	2,985.0	-96.0	2008 est.
116	North Korea	2,880.0	2,980.0	-100.0	2005
117	Mozambique	2,786.0	3,108.0	-322.0	2008 est.
118	Uganda	2,720.0	3,050.0	-330.0	2008 est.
119	Namibia	2,668.0	2,896.0	-228.0	2008 est
120	Honduras	2,628.0	3,183.0	-555.0	2008 est.
121	Armenia	2,438.0	2,696.0	-258.0	2008 est.
122	Chad	2,142.0	2,125.0	+17.0	2008 est.
123	Moldova	1,950.0	2,010.0	-60.0	2008
124	Mauritius	1,866.0	2,243.0	-377.0	2008 est.
125	Burkina Faso	1,799.0	2,337.0	-538.0	2008 est.
126	Mongolia	1,710.0	1,950.0	-240.0	2008
127	Nepal	1,700.0	2,300.0	-600.0	FY08
128	Madagascar	1,688.0	2,066.0	-378.0	2008 est.
129	Mali	1,500.0	1,800.0	-300.0	2006 est.
130	Benin	1,436.0	1,729.0	-293.0	2008 est.
131	Turkmenistan	1,393.0	1,420.0	-27.0	2008 est.
132	Fiji	1,363.0	1,376.0	-13.0	2006
—	Greenland	1,360.0	1,270.0	+90.0	2005
133	Tajikistan	1,280.0	1,300.0	-20.0	2008 est.

134	Nicaragua	1,271.0	1,593.0	-322.0	2008 est.
135	Cambodia	1,264.0	1,478.0	-214.0	2008 est.
136	Malawi	1,227.0	1,337.0	-110.0	2008 est.
137	Swaziland	1,215.0	1,155.0	+60.0	2008 est.
—	Template:Country data Kosovo under UNSCR1244/99	1,190.0	1,220.0	-30.0	2007 est.
138	Kyrgyzstan	1,170.0	1,192.0	-22.0	2008 est.
—	West Bank	1,149.0	2,310.0	-1,161.0	2006
—	Gaza Strip	1,149.0	2,310.0	-1,161.0	2006
139	Bahamas	1,030.0	1,030.0	+0.0	FY04/05
—	New Caledonia	996.0	1,072.0	-76.0	2001 est.
140	Burma	983.6	1,775.0	-791.4	2008 est.
—	Isle of Man	965.0	943.0	+22.0	FY05/06 est.
141	Rwanda	902.2	1,032.0	-129.8	2008 est.
142	Afghanistan	890.0	2,700.0	-1,810.0	2007 est.
—	French Polynesia	865.0	644.1	+220.9	1999
143	Monaco	863.0	920.6	-57.6	2005 est.
144	Barbados	847.0	886.0	-39.0	2000 est.
—	U.S. Virgin Islands	837.0	837.0	+0.0	FY08/09
—	Jersey	829.0	851.0	-22.0	2005
145	Haiti	820.6	965.2	-144.6	2008 est.
146	Laos	809.6	954.0	-144.4	2008 est.
147	Mauritania	770.0	770.0	+0.0	2007 est.
148	Maldives	762.0	884.0	-122.0	2008 est.
—	Netherlands Antilles	757.9	949.5	-191.6	2004
—	Bermuda	738.0	665.0	+73.0	FY04/05
149	Timor-Leste	733.0	309.0	+424.0	FY06/07 est.
150	Democratic Republic of the Congo	700.0	2,000.0	-1,300.0	2006 est.
151	San Marino	690.6	652.9	+37.7	2006
—	Faroe Islands	588.0	623.0	-35.0	2005
—	Guernsey	563.6	530.9	+32.7	2005
152	Togo	551.5	620.1	-68.6	2008 est.
153	Cape Verde	525.4	585.3	-59.9	2008 est.
154	Lesotho	523.0	479.5	+43.5	2008 est.
—	Aruba	507.9	577.9	-70.0	2005 est.
155	Andorra	496.9	496.8	+0.1	2007
156	Guyana	463.7	536.0	-72.3	2008 est.
—	Gibraltar	455.1	423.6	+31.5	2005 est.

157	Liechtenstein	424.2	414.1	+10.1	1998 est.
—	Cayman Islands	423.8	392.6	+31.2	2004
—	Mayotte	420.0	394.0	+26.0	2005
158	Suriname	392.6	425.9	-33.3	2004
159	Belize	335.5	361.5	-26.0	2008 est.
160	Niger	320.0	320.0	+0.0	2002 est.
—	Guam	319.6	427.8	-108.2	2002 est.
161	Seychelles	318.1	324.6	-6.5	2008 est.
162	Guinea	315.0	796.5	-481.5	2008 est.
163	Vatican City	310.0	307.0	+3.0	2006
164	Burundi	292.2	351.3	-59.1	2008 est.
165	Bhutan	272.0	350.0	-78.0	2005
166	Central African Republic	250.0	273.0	-23.0	2007 est.
167	Eritrea	234.5	523.1	-288.6	2008 est.
—	British Virgin Islands	204.7	180.4	+24.3	2004
168	Gambia	194.3	228.8	-34.5	2008 est
—	Northern Mariana Islands	193.0	223.0	-30.0	FY01/02 est.
169	Samoa	171.3	78.1	+93.2	FY04/05 est.
170	Federated States of Micronesia	166.0	152.7	+13.3	FY07 est.
—	American Samoa	155.4	183.6	-28.2	FY07
171	Saint Lucia	141.2	146.7	-5.5	2000 est.
172	Djibouti	135.0	182.0	-47.0	1999 est.
173	Antigua and Barbuda	123.7	145.9	-22.2	2000 est.
174	Marshall Islands	123.3	1,213.0	-1,089.7	2008
175	Palau	114.8	99.5	+15.3	2008 est.
176	Sierra Leone	96.0	351.0	-255.0	2000 est.
177	Saint Vincent and the Grenadines	94.6	85.8	+8.8	2000 est.
178	Saint Kitts and Nevis	89.7	128.2	-38.5	2003 est.
179	Grenada	85.8	102.1	-16.3	1997
180	Tonga	80.48	109.8	-29.32	FY07/08
181	Vanuatu	78.7	72.23	+6.47	2005
182	Dominica	73.9	84.4	-10.5	2001
—	Cook Islands	70.95	69.05	+1.9	FY05/06
—	Saint Pierre and Miquelon	70.0	60.0	+10.0	1996 est.
—	Falkland Islands	66.2	67.9	-1.7	FY98/99 est.
183	Kiribati	55.52	59.71	-4.19	FY05
184	Solomon Islands	49.7	75.1	-25.4	2003
185	Sao Tome and Principe	47.65	51.48	-3.83	2008 est.
—	Turks and Caicos Islands	47.0	33.6	+13.4	1997-98 est

—	Montserrat	31.4	31.6	-0.2	1997 est.
—	Anguilla	22.8	22.5	+0.3	2000 est.
186	Tuvalu	21.54	23.05	-1.51	2006
—	Niue	15.07	16.33	-1.26	FY0405
187	Nauru	13.5	13.5	+0.0	2005
—	Saint Helena	12.33	30.28	-17.95	FY06/07 est.
—	Norfolk Island	4.6	4.8	-0.2	FY99/00
—	Pitcairn Islands	0.746	1.028	-0.282	FY04/05
—	Tokelau	0.4308	2.8	-2.3692	1987 est.
188	Zimbabwe	0.1537	0.1793	-0.0256	2008 est.
—	Wallis and Futuna	0.02973	0.03133	-0.0016	2004

REFERENCES

B.E.V. Sabine (2006). *A History of Income Tax*. Taylor and Francis. pp. 230.

BBC News (1998-11-26). "What was in Norman Lamont's Budget box?". BBC. http://news.bbc.co.uk./1/hi/uk_politics/222610.stm

Brazilian Federal Budget: 2009 Chamber of Deputies of Brazil. Retrieved on 2009-08-04. (Portuguese)

David Boothroyd. "Political Television 1936–1955". *Political Television*. Demon Internet. http://www.election.demon.co.uk./pt1.html. Retrieved 2008-10-09.

Emrys Hughes (1962). *Macmillan: Portrait of a Politician*. London: G. Allen & Unwin.

John Biffen (1989). *Inside the House of Commons*. Grafton. pp. 127.

Mervyn A. King and Mark H. Robson (1993). "United Kingdom". in Dale Weldeau Jorgenson and Ralph Landau. *Tax Reform and the Cost of Capital*. Brookings Institution Press. pp. 300.

Nigel Lawson (1992). *The View from No. 11: Memoirs of a Tory Radical*. Bantam. pp. 326.

Rodney Brazier (1997). *Ministers of the Crown*. Oxford University Press. pp. 151–152,346.

Roland Arnold Young (1962). *The British Parliament*. Faber and Faber. pp. 170.

Sullivan, Arthur; Steven M. Sheffrin (2003). *Economics: Principles in action*. Upper Saddle River, New Jersey 07458: Pearson Prentice Hall. pp. 502.

Sullivan, Arthur; Steven M. Sheffrin (2003). *Economics: Principles in action*. Upper Saddle River, New Jersey 07458: Pearson Prentice Hall. pp. 376,403.

U.S. Constitution, Article 1, Sections 7-8.

Vickrey, William (October 5th, 1996), *Fifteen Fatal Fallacies of Financial Fundamentalism: A Disquisition on Demand Side Economics*, http://www.columbia.edu/dlc/wp/econ/vickrey.html. Paper was written one week before the author's death, three days before he received the Nobel Memorial Prize in Economics.

Walter Hines Page and Arthur Wilson Page (1916). *The World's Work ....: A History of Our Time*. New York: Doubleday, Page & Co.. pp. 190.

What is Finance?

Since finance is key factor in everyday life functioning, it is important to understand what is finance for every curious reader.

In fact, finance is the science of funds management The general areas of finance are *business finance*, *personal finance*, and *public finance*. Finance includes saving money and often includes lending money. The field of finance deals with the concepts of time, money, and risk and how they are interrelated. It also deals with how money is spent and budgeted.

Remarkably, one aspect of finance is through individuals and business organizations, which deposit money in a bank. The bank then lends the money out to other individuals or corporations for consumption or investment, and charges interest on the loans. Loans have become increasingly packaged for resale, meaning that an investor buys the loan (debt) from a bank or directly from a corporation. Bonds are debt instruments sold to investors for organizations such as companies, governments or charities. The investor can then hold the debt and collect the interest or sell the debt on a secondary market. Banks are the main facilitators of funding through the provision of credit, although private equity, mutual funds, hedge funds, and other organizations have become important as they invest in various forms of debt.

Financial assets, known as investments, are financially managed with careful attention to financial risk management to control financial risk. Financial instruments allow many forms of securitized assets to be traded on securities exchanges such as stock exchanges, including debt such as bonds as well as equity in publicly traded corporations. Central banks, such as the Federal Reserve System banks in the United States and Bank of England in the United Kingdom, are strong players in public finance, acting as lenders of last resort as well as strong influences on monetary and credit conditions in the economy.

An entity whose income exceeds their expenditure can lend or invest the excess income. On the other hand, an entity whose income is less than its expenditure can raise capital by borrowing or selling equity claims, decreasing its expenses, or increasing its income. The lender can find a borrower, a financial intermediary such as a bank, or buy notes or bonds in the bond market. The lender receives interest, the borrower pays a higher interest than the lender receives, and the financial intermediary pockets the difference.

A bank aggregates the activities of many borrowers and lenders. A bank accepts deposits from lenders, on which it pays interest. The bank then lends these deposits to borrowers. Banks allow borrowers and lenders, of different sizes, to coordinate their activity. Banks are thus compensators of money flows in space. A specific example of corporate finance is the sale of stock by a company to institutional investors like investment banks, who may sell it on to private investors, or other financial institutions such as pension funds. The stock give part ownership in that company in proportion to shares owned. In return for the stock, the company receives cash, which it may use to expand its business; ("equity financing"), to reduce its debt.

Equity financing mixed with the sale of bonds (or any other debt financing) is called the company's capital structure. Finance is used by individuals (personal finance), by governments (public finance), by businesses (corporate finance), as well as by a wide variety of organizations including schools and non-profit organizations. In general, the goals of each of the above activities are achieved through the use of appropriate financial instruments and methodologies, with consideration to their institutional setting. Finance is one of the most important aspects of business management. Without proper financial planning a new enterprise is unlikely to be successful. Managing money (a liquid asset) is essential to ensure a secure future, both for the individual and an organization

Personal Finance

Questions in personal finance revolve around:

- How much money will be needed by an individual (or by a family), and when?
- Where will this money come from, and how?
- How can people protect themselves against unforeseen personal events, as well as those in the external economy?
- How can family assets best be transferred across generations (bequests and inheritance)?
- How does tax policy (tax subsidies or penalties)

affect personal financial decisions?

- How does credit affect an individual's financial standing?
- How can one plan for a secure financial future in an environment of economic instability?

Personal financial decisions may involve paying for education, financing durable goods such as real estate and cars, buying insurance, e.g. health and property insurance, investing and saving for retirement.

Personal financial decisions may also involve paying for a loan, or debt obligations.

Corporate Finance

Managerial or corporate finance is the task of providing the funds for a corporation's activities. For small business, this is referred to as SME finance (Small and Medium Enterprises). It generally involves balancing risk and profitability, while attempting to maximize an entity's wealth and the value of its stock. Long term funds are provided by ownership equity and long-term credit, often in the form of bonds. The balance between these elements forms the company's capital structure. Short-term funding or working capital is mostly provided by banks extending a line of credit.

Another business decision concerning finance is investment, or fund management. An investment is an acquisition of an asset in the hope that it will maintain or increase its value. In investment management – in choosing a portfolio – one has to decide *what*, *how much* and *when* to invest.

To do this, a company must:

- Identify relevant objectives and constraints: institution or individual goals, time horizon, risk aversion and tax considerations;
- Identify the appropriate strategy: active *v*. passive – hedging strategy
- Measure the portfolio performance

Financial management is duplicate with the financial function of the Accounting profession. However, financial accounting is more concerned with the reporting of historical financial information, while the financial decision is directed toward the future of the firm.

Capital

Capital, in the financial sense, is the money that gives the business the power to buy goods to be used in the production of other goods or the offering of a service.

The desirability of budgeting: Budget is a document which documents the plan of the business. This may include the objective of business, targets set, and results in financial terms, e.g., the target set for sale, resulting cost, growth, required investment to achieve the planned sales, and financing source for the investment. Also budget may be long term or short term. Long term budgets have a time horizon of 5–10 years giving a vision to the company; short term is an annual budget which is drawn to control and operate in that particular year.

Capital Budget

This concerns proposed fixed asset requirements and how these expenditures will be financed. Capital budgets are often adjusted annually and should be part of a longer-term Capital Improvements Plan.

Cash Budget

Working capital requirements of a business should be monitored at all times to ensure that there are sufficient funds available to meet short-term expenses.

The cash budget is basically a detailed plan that shows all expected sources and uses of cash. The cash budget has the following six main sections:

1. Beginning Cash Balance - contains the last period's closing cash balance.
2. Cash collections - includes all expected cash receipts (all sources of cash for the period considered, mainly sales)
3. Cash disbursements - lists all planned cash outflows for the period, excluding interest payments on short-term loans, which appear in the financing section. All expenses that do not affect cash flow are excluded from this list (e.g. depreciation, amortization, etc.)
4. Cash excess or deficiency - a function of the cash needs and cash available. Cash needs are determined by the total cash disbursements plus the minimum cash balance required by company policy. If total cash available is less than cash needs, a deficiency exists.
5. Financing - discloses the planned borrowings and repayments, including interest.
6. Ending Cash balance - simply reveals the planned ending cash balance.

Management of Current Assets

Credit Policy

Credit gives the consumer the opportunity to buy,

purchase or acquire goods and services, and pay for them at a later date. This has its advantages and disadvantages as follows:

Advantages of Credit Trade

- Usually results in more customers than cash trade.
- Can charge more for goods to cover the risk of bad debt.
- Gain goodwill and loyalty of customers.
- People can buy goods and pay for them at a later date.
- Farmers can buy seeds and implements, and pay for them only after the harvest.
- Stimulates agricultural and industrial production and commerce.
- Can be used as a promotional tool.
- Increase the sales.
- Modest rates to be filled.
- can be a marketing tool

Disadvantages of Credit Trade

- Risk of bad debt.
- High administration expenses.
- People can buy more than they can afford.
- More working capital needed.
- Risk of Bankruptcy.
- May lose peace of mind.

Forms of Credit

- Suppliers credit:

- Credit on ordinary open account
- Installment sales
- Bills of exchange
- Credit cards
- Contractor's credit
- Factoring of debtors
- Cash credit
- Cpf credits
- Exchange of product

Factors Which Influence Credit Conditions

- Nature of the business's activities
- Financial position
- Product durability
- Length of production process
- Competition and competitors' credit conditions
- Country's economic position
- Conditions at financial institutions
- Discount for early payment
- Debtor's type of business and financial position

Credit Collection

Overdue Accounts

- Attach a notice of overdue account to statement.
- Send a letter asking for settlement of debt.
- Send a second or third letter it first is ineffectual.
- Threaten legal actions.

Effective Credit Control

- Increases sales
- Reduces bad debts
- Increases profits
- Builds customer loyalty
- Builds confidence of financial industry
- Increase company capitalisation
- Increase the customer relationship

Sources of Information on Creditworthiness

- Business references
- Bank references
- Credit agencies
- Chambers of commerce
- Employers
- Credit application forms

Duties of the Credit Department

- Legal action
- Taking necessary steps to ensure settlement of account
- Knowing the credit policy and procedures for credit control
- Setting credit limits
- Ensuring that statements of account are sent out
- Ensuring that thorough checks are carried out on credit customers
- Keeping records of all amounts owing
- Ensuring that debts are settled promptly

- Timely reporting to the upper level of management for better management.

Stock

Purpose of Stock Control

- Ensures that enough stock is on hand to satisfy demand.
- Protects and monitors theft.
- Safeguards against having to stockpile.
- Allows for control over selling and cost price.

Stockpiling

This refers to the purchase of stock at the right time, at the right price and in the right quantities.

There are several advantages to the stockpiling, the following are some of the examples:

- Losses due to price fluctuations and stock loss kept to a minimum
- Ensures that goods reach customers timeously; better service
- Saves space and storage cost
- Investment of working capital kept to minimum
- No loss in production due to delays

There are several disadvantages to the stockpiling, the following are some of the examples:

- Obsolescence
- Danger of fire and theft
- Initial working capital investment is very large
- Losses due to price fluctuation

Rate of Stock Turnover

This refers to the number of times per year that the average level of stock is sold. It may be worked out by dividing the cost price of goods sold by the cost price of the average stock level.

Determining Optimum Stock Levels

- Maximum stock level refers to the maximum stock level that may be maintained to ensure cost effectiveness.
- Minimum stock level refers to the point below which the stock level may not go.
- Standard order refers to the amount of stock generally ordered.
- Order level refers to the stock level which calls for an order to be made.

Cash

Reasons for Keeping Cash

- Cash is usually referred to as the "king" in finance, as it is the most liquid asset.
- The transaction motive refers to the money kept available to pay expenses.
- The precautionary motive refers to the money kept aside for unforeseen expenses.
- The speculative motive refers to the money kept aside to take advantage of suddenly arising opportunities.

Advantages of Sufficient Cash

- Current liabilities may be catered for meeting the current obligations of the company

- Cash discounts are given for cash payments.
- Production is kept moving
- Surplus cash may be invested on a short-term basis.
- The business is able to pay its accounts in a timely manner, allowing for easily obtained credit.
- Liquidity
- Quick upfront pay.

Management of Fixed Assets

Depreciation

Depreciation is the allocation of the cost of an asset over its useful life as determined at the time of purchase. It is calculated yearly to enforce the matching principle.

Insurance

Insurance is the undertaking of one party to indemnify another, in exchange for a premium, against a certain eventuality.

Uninsured Risks

- Bad debt
- Changes in fashion
- Time lapses between ordering and delivery
- New machinery or technology
- Different prices at different places

Requirements of an Insurance Contract

- Insurable interest
  - The insured must derive a real financial gain from that which he is insuring, or stand to lose if it is destroyed or lost.

  - The item must belong to the insured.
  - One person may take out insurance on the life of another if the second party owes the first money.
  - Must be some person or item which can, legally, be insured.
  - The insured must have a legal claim to that which he is insuring.
- Good faith
  - *Uberrimae fidei* refers to absolute honesty and must characterise the dealings of both the insurer and the insured.

Shared Services

There is currently a move towards converging and consolidating Finance provisions into shared services within an organization. Rather than an organization having a number of separate Finance departments performing the same tasks from different locations a more centralized version can be created.

Finance of States

Country, state, county, city or municipality finance is called public finance. It is concerned with

- Identification of required expenditure of a public sector entity
- Source(s) of that entity's revenue
- The budgeting process
- Debt issuance (municipal bonds) for public works projects

Financial Economics

Financial economics is the branch of economics studying the interrelation of financial variables, such as prices, interest rates and shares, as opposed to those concerning the real economy. Financial economics concentrates on influences of real economic variables on financial ones, in contrast to pure finance.

It studies:

- Valuation - Determination of the fair value of an asset
  - How risky is the asset? (identification of the asset-appropriate discount rate)
  - What cash flows will it produce? (discounting of relevant cash flows)
  - How does the market price compare to similar assets? (relative valuation)
  - Are the cash flows dependent on some other asset or event? (derivatives, contingent claim valuation)
- Financial markets and instruments
  - Commodities - topics
  - Stocks - topics
  - Bonds - topics
  - Money market instruments- topics
  - Derivatives - topics
- Financial institutions and regulation

Financial Econometrics is the branch of Financial Economics that uses econometric techniques to parameterise the relationships.

Financial Mathematics

Financial mathematics is a main branch of applied mathematics concerned with the financial markets. Financial mathematics is the study of financial data with the tools of mathematics, mainly statistics. Such data can be movements of securities—stocks and bonds etc.—and their relations. Another large subfield is insurance mathematics. This is also known as quantitative finance, practitioners as Quantitative analysts.

Experimental Finance

Experimental finance aims to establish different market settings and environments to observe experimentally and provide a lens through which science can analyze agents' behavior and the resulting characteristics of trading flows, information diffusion and aggregation, price setting mechanisms, and returns processes. Researchers in experimental finance can study to what extent existing financial economics theory makes valid predictions, and attempt to discover new principles on which such theory can be extended. Research may proceed by conducting trading simulations or by establishing and studying the behaviour of people in artificial competitive market-like settings.

Behavioral Finance

Behavioral Finance studies how the psychology of investors or managers affects financial decisions and markets. Behavioral finance has grown over the last few decades to become central to finance.

Behavioral finance includes such topics as:

1. Empirical studies that demonstrate significant deviations from classical theories.

2. Models of how psychology affects trading and prices
3. Forecasting based on these methods.
4. Studies of experimental asset markets and use of models to forecast experiments.

A strand of behavioral finance has been dubbed Quantitative Behavioral Finance, which uses mathematical and statistical methodology to understand behavioral biases in conjunction with valuation. Some of this endeavor has been led by Gunduz Caginalp (Professor of Mathematics and Editor of Journal of Behavioral Finance during 2001-2004) and collaborators including Vernon Smith (2002 Nobel Laureate in Economics), David Porter, Don Balenovich, Vladimira Ilieva, Ahmet Duran). Studies by Jeff Madura, Ray Sturm and others have demonstrated significant behavioral effects in stocks and exchange traded funds. Among other topics, quantitative behavioral finance studies behavioral effects together with the non-classical assumption of the finiteness of assets.

Intangible Asset Finance

Intangible asset finance is the area of finance that deals with intangible assets such as patents, trademarks, goodwill, reputation, etc.

3

Fundamentals of Budget Preparation

Institutional Mechanisms for Policy Formulation

To start with, an overall strategic framework should underpin the formulation of sectoral policies provided that it is a genuine and concrete strategy, rather than a generic "mission statement", or rhetorical vision. Within this framework, line ministries and agencies could prepare their own strategic plans, including: (i) their mandate, consistent with statutory requirements; (ii) a set of outcomes; (iii) the approaches to achieving these outcomes; (iv) a description of how activities and process will be used to achieve these objectives; and (v) a broad cost estimate. Performance plans can then be derived for these strategic plans. Such strategic planning is not a static exercise or an occasional event, but a dynamic and inclusive process. If done well, strategic planning is continuous and provides the basis for everything the organization does each day.

Regrettably, in many cases the exercise degenerates into bureaucratic formalism, where matrices, long-term vision and logical frameworks substitute for clear thinking rather than being used as instruments to make it explicit. A good practical rule in preparing (and evaluating) a strategic framework is: keep it simple.

It is pertinent to note that there is no blueprint for the organizational arrangements for policy formulation. In all cases however, the relationship between government levels must be established by law. The common requirement is that they must ensure coherence and close coordination among the different actors. The "center of government", i.e., depending on the country, the Prime Minister's office, the President's office, etc., should coordinate the policy formulation process. It must be able to set up policy priorities, coordinate interministerial committees, act as arbiter, launch and coordinate the preparation of strategic plans by sector ministries (or intersectoral committees for cross-cutting policy issues). The center of government therefore needs strategic planning capacity, which could consist of a small group of advisers relieved of day-to-day government coordination activities (but systematically in contact with the operational organs). In several developing countries, a dual policy decision-making process exists, since government is coordinated both by the President's office and the Prime Minister's office. In these cases, a clear demarcation of their respective roles is needed. Line ministries should be responsible for policy making within their portfolios.

This obvious principle bears underlining because it is so often violated—either by excessive intervention from the center on sector policy issues, or from the Ministry of Finance on sector budget issues, or from the Ministry of Planning when selecting sectoral projects included in the investment program or from donors lobbying in favor of pet projects, and/or from the line ministry itself seeking to evade responsibility by using any of the above as excuses.

The effectiveness of the line minister in coordinating sector policy can also be impeded by internal organizational arrangements within the line ministry itself. Thus, for example, in countries where substantial cuts have been made in the ministry's own current and investment budget, an autonomous fund that benefits from earmarked revenues or a state-owned enterprise in the sector can be much more powerful than the relevant minister.

In fact, policy formulation can to an extent be separated from the delivery of the corresponding services. This can help avoid "capture" of the policy function by vested administrative interests. Moreover, in many developing and transition countries, decoupling policy advice from service delivery, without giving increased resources to the central departments responsible for policy advice, makes for fragmentation and inconsistency in the formulation of sector policies, since in effect these policies end up being formulated by the entities responsible for delivering the services. The typical outcome is that the Ministry of Finance deals directly with the service delivery entities when preparing the budget and the line ministry is barely involved or even informed—a different variant of "capture".

To cite an example, Australia has been successful in implementing super-ministries ("portfolio ministries"). These portfolio ministries were made responsible for defining priorities in their respective sectors under tight resource constraints. This organizational arrangement facilitates adjustments in the composition of expenditure programs. Putting complementary programs under one portfolio highlights the need for trade-offs and gives room to finance new priorities through offsetting savings, while complying with the resource constraint. However, in other countries, a super-ministry could simply be the a grouping of "junior" ministries, adding an unnecessary layer of decision making to the machinery of government, tending to make policy formulation more complex. Interministerial committees are needed to deal with cross-cutting policy issues (e.g., employment, environment), to coordinate policy areas that are covered by several ministries; or deal with special problems (e.g., regional issues). Setting up task forces can be a flexible way to tackle some special issues, provided that a specific sunset clause—is set and resolutely enforced. The administrative landscape in most countries contains several such entities, still surviving long after the need for their establishment has disappeared.

A cohesive civil service "culture" is important for policy coordination. Especially, problematic are systems where mobility is constrained not only by the usual obstacles, but also by the existence of several different professional "streams" with no possibility of moving between them. Normally, a system whereby officials move among ministries is better able to produce policy coordination than a system in which civil servants spend most of their careers in the same ministry.

However, in cases where government is weak across the board and civil servants are incompetent or corrupt, greater mobility may simply serve to generalize incompetence or corruption, eliminate "pockets" of efficiency or honesty, and make reform that much harder. Circulation of information within the government is crucial. Because it is often seen as an asset to be traded, *information will simply not flow by itself*. Formal and robust mechanisms are needed to ensure it, such as systematic consultation with other ministries, clear rules for circulation of draft decisions before Cabinet meeting, guidelines for documenting decisions, appropriate rewards or penalties. But restraint must be exercised to keep communications relevant and avoid the information overload that hampers genuine communication almost as much as inadequacy of information. Committees dealing with cross-cutting issues at different administrative levels generally facilitate the circulation of information, but must not be allowed to dilute the line ministries' responsibility in their own areas.

BOX 1

Key Prerequisites for Well-Functioning Cabinet Systems

An ADB study analyzed cabinet processes and procedures in six countries—Australia, Great Britain, Malaysia, Philippines, Singapore and Sri Lanka. It defined four broad criteria for good cabinet performance: efficiency, effectiveness, accountability and transparency.

The study showed that Cabinet systems seem to be more effective where:

- Extensive interministerial coordination takes place when proposals are prepared;
- Implementation of Cabinet decisions is tracked, through monitoring or other follow-up systems;
- Budgetary resources for implementing Cabinet policies are identified at an early stage of the policy process;
- The Cabinet as a whole takes and stands by decisions collectively;
- The Secretary to the Cabinet (or equivalent position) has the trust and confidence of the Prime Minister or President;
- The staff of the Cabinet/Secretariat is composed of highly respected, competent, experienced, and discrete professionals;
- Ministers and their Permanent Secretaries communicate openly and regularly;
- The number of Cabinet ministers is small, thus simplifying the task of coordination. Leaner Cabinets tend to allow for greater policy cohesion, as well as more efficient meetings;

- Cabinet business forecasting systems are in place;
- The cabinet agenda is limited to a few tough decision items; other routine or lowpriority decisions are delegated to permanent secretaries and other line ministry officials;
- Real deliberation over most policy issues has taken place at the committee level before the issue is brought to the full Cabinet for ratification;
- Cabinet memoranda are well-written and concise, with clearly stated objectives and recommendations;
- Cabinet meeting minutes which briefly summarize decisions are conveyed clearly and quickly;
- Cabinet office or other staff brief the meeting's Chairperson (President or PM, or Minister, in the case of committee meetings) before each meeting;
- Cabinet office staff are motivated and regulated according to professional standards;
- Policy proposals are presented as multiple or preferred choices for decision by elected officials rather than as single options recommended without alternative by appointed officials;
- Extensive consultation on policy issues takes place among politicians and technocrats in both formal and informal settings;
- Mechanisms for public consultation are established;
- Written procedures guide the preparation of policy proposals and the implementation of policy decisions, and these procedures are open to public scrutiny; and
- The Cabinet office (or another part of the head of state's office) ensures that the government communicates clearly to the public the rationale for important and/or controversial policy decisions.

[**Source:** Asian Development Bank, Case studies on central mechanisms for policy formulation, coordination and implementation in the Asia Pacific region (RETA 5685), June 1998.]

Particularly, formal and clear communication and clearance channels are important to avoid implementation problems and misunderstanding, particularly in countries where personalized networks are important. The Cabinet must clearly be the locus where decisions are made; initiatives from ministries should be submitted to the center of government; initiatives that affect the public finances to the Ministry of Finance; and decisions must be systematically documented and formally communicated.

Distribution of Responsibilities for the Macroeconomic Framework

In general practice, preparing macroeconomic projections should involve directly the agencies responsible for macroeconomic issues, normally the Ministry of Finance, the Central Bank, the Treasury Department, the Ministry of Planning (if any), the Statistics Bureau, and, as the occasion requires, sector ministries. In some countries, a single agency is responsible for preparing of the macroeconomic framework (with the Central Bank normally responsible for its own monetary and balance-of-payments projections). In other countries, the responsibility for macroeconomic projections is fragmented, with the Ministry of Finance responsible for fiscal projections, the Ministry of Planning for projections for the real sector, the Statistics Bureau for short-term projections for the real sector and price forecasts. In these cases, the macroeconomic projections are simply the collected forecasts from different agencies.

For administrative and bureaucratic reasons, whichever agency is responsible for putting together these forecasts is usually reluctant to amend them or to request revisions. The immediate result is lack of consistency of the projections and poor dialogue within the government on policy issues.

The indirect result is greater influence by the external financial institutions involved in financing the requirements of the adjustment program. When responsibility is fragmented, therefore, it is essential for the country's policy autonomy to set up an inter-ministerial committee with the authority to scrutinize the different sets of projections, assess their realism and consistency, and require changes—with the assistance of a competent technical secretariat. Another problematic situation arises when the agency responsible for the preparation of the macroeconomic framework is separated from the entity responsible for overall budget management.

The argument in favor of such an arrangement is that it relieves the agency responsible for the macroeconomic framework from the pressures of day-to-day administration of the budget, thus allowing medium-term strategy to be better taken into account. In practice, however, this often disconnects the preparation of the macroeconomic framework from immediate issues, and transforms it into a pro-forma exercise, while the real issues are addressed elsewhere (typically during meetings between the IMF and the Central Bank and the Ministry of Finance). Understandably, this encourages a mechanistic and lackadaisical attitude to macroeconomic projections, and the tendency to blame difficulties with budget implementation on the poor quality of someone else's forecasts.

It is pertinent to note that developing countries have been successful in establishing good coordination mechanisms for the formulation of macroeconomic policy. In other countries, whatever the distribution of responsibilities for preparing the official macroeconomic framework, the Ministry of Finance must have the internal capacity to review the macroeconomic projections, assess the risks associated with the different macroeconomic and fiscal scenarios, and prepare its own macroeconomic scenario to serve as a basis for comparison and reality check.

Distribution of Responsibilities in Annual Budget Preparation

Different actors are involved in budget preparation: the center of government, the Ministry of Finance (which consists of both the Ministry of Finance and the Ministry of Planning in many developing countries) central departments of line ministries and, within line ministries, subordinate spending agencies. The quality of the budget depends largely on the mode of coordination that is established among these different actors.

The distribution of responsibilities in budget preparation should fit the distribution of responsibilities within the government. It should be established in the budget rules or guidelines, along clear lines in order to establish unquestioned rules for compliance and accountability in budget execution. The organization of the executive branch of government in most countries suggests a distribution of responsibilities along the following lines:

1. The center of government is not directly involved in the practical aspects of budget preparation, but plays a key role in the budgetary process, to ensure that it is carried out along the lines defined and arbitrate and smooth over any conflict that may appear among the actors, and assure participation by the relevant stakeholders.
2. The Ministry of Finance has the leading role in budget preparation. It needs sufficient powers to ensure that both fiscal targets and policy objectives are taken into account at every step. It prepares

fiscal targets and strategic prioritization among sectors; establishes guidelines for preparing sector programs and for preparing line ministries' requests; scrutinizes those requests; and drafts the budget. However, the Ministry of Finance should not become the only player in the process. The budget should not drive policies. The Ministry of Finance has to facilitate decisions on major policy choices and allocation of resources among sectors, not make those decisions. The Ministry of Finance has to review and screen requests, not prepare them, directly or indirectly, as is the case in "open-ended" budget preparation and incremental budgeting.

3. Line ministries are responsible and accountable for defining and implementing government policies in their sector. Therefore, they should be responsible for developing sectoral policies and their sectoral budgets as well, but within the framework established by the government. Moreover, they (and not the center or the Ministry of Finance) should have the technical capacities and information needed for trade-offs among ongoing programs and appraise new programs. In turn, line ministries are responsible for formulating guidelines for their subordinate agencies and scrutinizing their draft budgets.

4. Subordinate agencies should prepare their budgets within the guidelines provided by their immediate direct authority. Often, powerful agencies prefer to deal directly with the Ministry of Finance; this hampers the definition of consistent sector policies.

Remarkably, most developed countries have organized the distribution of responsibilities in budget preparation along the above lines. In developing countries, by contrast, the role of the Ministry of Finance in budget preparation can be more extensive and can strongly interfere in the preparation and the composition of the sectoral budgets. In countries with poor governance, subordinate agencies may see the Ministry of Finance as a protector against the confiscation of resources by "advisers" to the minister or by the line ministry's central departments.3 The informal network of technicians from the Ministry of Finance and the line ministries may try to use the complexity of a line-item budget to protect some sectors or items. However understandable this may be, this defensive approach generally gives poor results. Bad policies and weak governance cannot be corrected at micro-level by insulating temporarily a specific budget line item or subordinate agency.

The Budget Timetable

1. Budget Circular: A budget circular generally introduces the budget preparation process to spending agencies. It is often a routine affair, giving deadlines for the presentation of line ministries' requests and some general recommendations.

For a sound budget preparation process, the budget circular should state clearly the fiscal targets and the policies proposed. Ideally, a budget circular should include the following elements:

- a statement of the macroeconomic and financial situation;
- the overall deficit target and expected resources;
- budget priorities;
- sectoral budget ceilings;
- allocations for continuing policies and programs (for this, a rolling expenditure programming process is required);

- an indication of the expenditure savings expected in ongoing programs;
- the format of the line ministries' budget requests (presentation of sector policy, performance indicators, etc.);
- specific recommendations on program/projects;
- guidelines for the preparation of the sector programs (i.e., minimum requirement in terms of economic analysis to support a proposed investment project);
- economic parameters such as the expected inflation rate and the exchange rate;
- the organization of the budget preparation process (calendar, forms to be completed, etc.).

2. Budget Preparation Calendar: For sufficient iteration between the top-down and the bottom-up approach, adequate time is needed, notably to allow line ministries to prepare their budgets and identify measures to comply with the ceilings.

Remarkably, in several developed countries, the budget circular for the next year is sent to spending agencies soon after the start of each fiscal year. Therefore, budget preparation starts nine to ten months before the budget is presented to the legislature. In the United States, taking into account the special role of Congress, the budget preparation takes about 18 months. In some developing countries, budget preparation is sometimes starts early but the sectoral ceilings are announced much later, and across-the-board cuts or arbitrary choices have to be made at the last minute. The optimal length of the budget calendar is difficult to establish, and depends on the country context.

On the one hand, a short calendar (or a short time between the notification of ceilings and the deadline for presentation of the budget requests) does not allow line ministries and subordinate agencies to prepare their program properly, or leaves no time for the needed negotiations.

On the other hand, a lengthy process could lead to a budget based on out-of-date estimates of economic and fiscal parameters, which in addition could not take into account the results of the execution of the previous year's budget.

Unfortunately, countries with unstable and hard-to-forecast parameters (such as high-inflation countries) are precisely those countries that need more time to make the hard choices among their programs. Generally, a budget preparation period starting six months before the deadline for presentation of the budget to the legislature is appropriate in developing countries, but there is no hard rule, and no substitute for custom-tailoring the budget calendar to the specific country.

RESPONSIBILITIES BETWEEN CENTRAL AND LOCAL GOVERNMENT

Certain key issues related to the fiscal relationship between national and subnational levels of government must be considered. In fact, each governmental entity (central government, states, municipalities, etc.) should have its own budget, enacted according to the provisions stipulated in the Constitution or by law. However, there are strong linkages between the budget of the central government and the budgets of subnational governments, which require particular attention when preparing the budget of the central government.

BOX 2

Possible Timetable for Budget Preparation

Month	*Phase*
T-8	The macroeconomic framework is prepared.
T-7	Ceilings are determined by sector (for the annual budget *and, if prepared, MYE or PIP*); Cabinet approves strategy.
T-6	Budget circular is released.
T-4	Line ministries submit budget *(with forward cost estimates)*
T-3	Budget requests are reviewed and negotiated between MOF and individual line ministries *(and MYE or PIP). In dual budgeting systems, reviews are made jointly* by MOF and Ministry of Planning.
T-1	Budget is submitted to the legislature
T	Month when budget is approved by legislature

Partly drawn from Guidance for Fiscal Economists on Public Expenditure Management, FAD.

Major Issues in "Fiscal Federalism"

The degree of devolution, assignment of expenditures and revenue arrangements should be tailored to the country context and depend on policy and political issues. However, central government budget managers need to be aware of the key principles that should govern these arrangements.

From an efficiency perspective, the Oates "decentralization theorem" states that: "each public service should be provided by the jurisdiction having control over the minimum geographic area that would internalize benefits and costs of such provision." Similarly, the European Union has adopted the "principle of subsidiarity", for the assignment of responsibilities among its members.

According to this principle, taxing, spending, and regulatory functions should be exercised by lower levels of government unless a convincing case can be made for assigning them to higher levels of government.

BOX 3

Fiscal Management in Federal Systems

In the 1980s, Argentina and Brazil faced similar problems, with subnational deficits adding to excess public deficits and high inflation. In the 1990s, both countries continued with fiscal decentralization and with the struggle to bring about macroeconomic stability. Argentina had greater success, partly because it imposed a harder budget constraint on the public sector at the national level and it had stronger party control of the subnational governments and of the national legislators. For restraining local and state borrowing, getting the right incentives for subnational governments and particularly for its creditors, in Argentina, proved more effective than central government rules, in Brazil (Steven Webb and William Dillinger, 1998).

In the People's Republic of China, the implementation of the Budget Law in 1994 strengthened the basis for fiscal operations. Central approval of local budgets was abolished, and budgetary procedures were clarified, requiring the local and central budgets to be formulated in a consistent macroeconomic framework. Local governments were disallowed from financing any deficits through bond issues, bank borrowing, or grants from the central government. They were required to run balanced budgets or to use accumulated budgetary surpluses and extrabudgetary funds to finance deficits (IMF WP/97/129).

Further, Decentralization is a very complex matter, both in general and for the management of public expenditure. It is generally desirable for efficiency, local accountability, and participation. These criteria must be balanced with other elements, such as spatial externalities, economies of scale, overall fiscal efficiency (e.g., more generous public services in one region would encourage people to move there, even if economic opportunities may not exist), regional equity, and the redistributive responsibilities of the government. In developing and transition countries, the administrative capacity of subnational governments, and the administrative and compliance costs of decentralization must be taken into account when assigning expenditures among levels of government. Political issues and, in a number of countries, ethnic or nationality problems cannot be ignored, either. The literature on fiscal federalism discusses these issues and gives hypothetical and real-life examples of expenditure assignment. It also presents various contradictory points of view on the desirable degree of decentralization. The need for some increased fiscal decentralization is generally admitted. Many observers, however, stress the risk of loss in expenditure control, increased corruption, and inefficiencies in resource allocation that would result from hasty decentralization, even when theoretically justified.

Notably, in any event, tax and revenue arrangements should be in conformity with expenditure assignments, and should take into account efficiency issues in tax administration. Such arrangements may include:

(i) tax assignment, i.e., assignment of certain taxes to subnational governments;

(ii) tax-sharing agreements;

(iii) revenue sharing, whereby a share of a pool of tax revenue is given to the subnational levels of government;

(iv) unconditional grants;

(v) conditional "block grants", i.e., transfers from the central government subject to certain conditions or standards of service delivery;

(vi) targeted grants for a specific purpose or project. Among the various possible alternatives, the Australian Grants Commission System has much to commend it. It has successfully equalized access to basic social services, while preserving the incentive of each state to provide the services more efficiently, and largely depoliticizing the contentious issue of federal-state revenue sharing.

Main Principles

Whatever the degree of devolution appropriate to the country, the framework that governs the relationships between the central and local governments and arrangements for budgeting should be clear and efficient. As noted at the outset, a legal framework should govern the relationship between the different levels of the government. However, it is impossible to provide for every situation in a codified law or contract. Conflict resolution mechanisms are therefore important to assure smooth intergovernmental fiscal relations. Such mechanisms could operate through specialized bodies. In India, Australia, and Sri Lanka, for example, a Financial Commission deals with financial relationships between the central government and the other levels of the government; in Germany, a second chamber of Parliament with state representation contributes to intergovernmental policy coordination; and specialized sectoral coordination councils are common in many countries.

For *transparency and efficiency of management*:

1. Each level of government should have clearly assigned

responsibilities, regardless of what those responsibilities are assigned to government as a whole. Overlaps should generally be avoided, and long "concurrent lists" of shared responsibilities are particularly ambiguous.

2. Fiscal and revenue-sharing arrangements between the central and local governments should be stable. They may be amended from time to time, but renewed bargaining each year should be avoided at all costs.

3. Subnational governments need to have a sound estimate of these resources before preparing their budgets. In some countries (e.g., Ukraine in 1996-97), local governments have to wait for the draft budget of the central government to be finalized before preparing their own budgets. Such lack of predictability hampers both efficiency and fiscal control at local levels. Without an indication of the level of resources to be transferred to them, subnational governments cannot adjust their expenditures to fiscal constraints. Accordingly, forecasts of revenues should be transmitted to local governments as soon as these are set, and estimates of grants to local governments need to be prepared early in the budget process of the central government.

4. Incentives for increased efficiency are needed. Often the central government makes transfers to subnational governments when they make economies in public spending or improve their own tax collection. This evidently does not stimulate them to seek economies in service delivery or improve tax collection. Subnational governments must be allowed to benefit from savings they make, at least in a large part.

BOX 4

Defining China's Expenditure Assignments

To date, China has failed to work out a law that clearly defines expenditure responsibilities for different levels of government. Existing expenditure assignments are murky, and often, motivated by political expediency, shift between levels of government in ad hoc ways. The central government may shift its own expenditure responsibilities to provincial governments in times of difficulty and provincial governments may use their broader responsibilities to bargain for a larger share of revenue. Intergovernmental bargaining has weakened budgetary planning and control and contributed to the instability of China's fiscal system. Without first reaching decisions on expenditure assignment, the Chinese authorities have found it difficult to reform tax assignment rules and revenue-sharing mechanisms between the central and provincial governments.

Expenditure assignments between the provincial government and lower-level authorities, such as municipal and county, are even more vague. Local governments are often forced to take the responsibility that should be undertaken by higher-level government, accentuating the mismatch between local revenue and local expenditure responsibility. The lack of specificity and the unpredictability built into the current system of expenditure assignments have given rise to budgetary uncertainty for the central government and made fiscal planning an impossible task for provincial and local authorities, hence adversely affecting the supply of public goods and services in both quantity and quality.

[**Source:** Reforming China's Public Finances, Ehtisham Ahmad, Gao Qiang & Vito Tanzi (editors), IMF, 1995.]

5. It could be desirable to agree on multi-year "contracts" between the central government and local governments covering both expenditure assignments and revenue arrangements (tax sharing, grants, etc.). These contracts could, if appropriate, include

performance criteria, minimum standards for services rendered by local government, etc. They would define relationships in a transparent manner and would ensure predictability. As for any contract, of course, the utility of this arrangement would depend largely on how well it is monitored and respected.

For *expenditure control and strategic allocation of resources*:

1. Fiscal targets should cover the *general* government.
2. Revenue assignment should be fully consistent with expenditure assignment. Sufficient resources should be assigned to subnational governments to allow them to fulfill their duties. When new duties or responsibilities are transferred to subnational governments, compensatory measures should be provided on the revenue side. On the other hand, of course, if some duties or responsibilities are removed, transfers to subnational government should be correspondingly reduced.
3. "Downloading" the fiscal deficit should not be permitted (defining fiscal targets for general government would help avoid this problem). When balancing its budget, the central government should avoid passing its financial problems to subnational governments through cuts in intergovernmental transfers or increased expenditure assignments, without compensatory measures. To do so would either not change the aggregate borrowing requirements of the *general* government, or generate arrears.

4. Special mechanisms are needed to control local government borrowing.

5. In case of local government budget overruns or accumulation of arrears, the law should stipulate sanctions or emergency measures. For example, local authorities could be forced to cut expenditures or raise taxes, or local budgets could be placed under the authority of the central government for a limited period of time until the situation is stabilized.

6 A sound reporting and accounting system is critical. Subnational government financial operations should be consolidated with central government operations. Systems for budget execution, internal control and audit for subnational governments should be similar to those of the central government. This leads one back to the central question of local government administrative capacity, and hence the issue of the degree of decentralization.

7. For policy analysis (as well as fiscal targets of general government), it is necessary to consolidate the expenditure of the different levels of government especially in decentralized systems and federal countries. It would be very difficult to know what is spent on key sectors based only on the account of the central government. For this purpose, local governments and central government should have a common functional and economic classification of expenditures.

BOX 5

Arrangements for Controlling Subnational Government Borrowing

Country	*Local and municipal authorities / Debt limits*
United States	All local governments must have a balanced budget. Most states have either a constitutional or a statutory requirement for a balanced budget.
Canada	No formal restrictions. Market mechanisms are in place.
United Kingdom	A balanced budget is required.
Sweden	A balanced budget is required. Local and municipal governments are responsible for their own debt.
Australia:	The Australian Debt Council determines the total public debt and the distribution between the different government levels, but in practice market mechanisms operate.
New Zealand	Generally speaking, local governments must finance current expenditures with revenues for the same year.
Argentina	The provinces may contract debt both internally and externally. The Central Bank oversees the impact on the financial system, and the Ministry of the Economy oversees maximum external interest rates.
Brazil	The Federal Senate sets overall limits to the amount of debt that states, the Federal District, and the municipalities can contract, and establishes the rules and conditions for their external and internal credit operations.
Chile	Municipalities and state-owned enterprises are able to contract loans for special projects. But this requires a law that must also indicate how the loan is to be repaid.
Colombia	According to constitutional regulations, local government's debts may not exceed their

	ability for repayment. A law is in place that establishes graduated authorization procedures according to debt levels.
Mexico	The states may not, in any case, directly or indirectly contract obligations or loans with foreign governments, companies, or private parties; or loans that must be repaid in foreign currency. States and municipalities may contract loans only when they are for productive public investments.
Venezuela	Local and municipal entities may not contract loans without the authorization of federal authorities.

[**Source:** Ter-Minassian, T. (1996) and Petrei, 1998.]

APPROVAL OF THE BUDGET AND THE LEGISLATURE

Presentation of the budget to the legislature

The enactment of the budget should not merely be a formal exercise carried out to comply with the Constitution. The legislature is, generally, the appropriate locus of overall financial accountability. Naturally, the role of the legislature should be to approve future actions rather than to rubber-stamp decisions already taken. Thus, the budget should be presented to the legislature in a timely manner, that is, two to four months before the start of the fiscal year, to allow budgetary debates to be completed before the start of the fiscal year. In some countries, the budget is submitted to the legislature after the start of the fiscal year, owing to unavoidable delays in budget preparation, change in the composition of the Cabinet, or pending financial negotiations with IFIs. However, in other countries, delay is institutionalized.

In Nepal, the budget is presented systematically to

Parliament only days before the beginning of the fiscal year. Therefore, Parliament has to authorize the government to spend immediately one-sixth of the appropriations presented in a Budget Bill that it has not yet scrutinized. In China, the National People's Congress (NPC) does not meet to approve the budget until after the commencement of the fiscal year. As a result, it is asked to approve appropriations for a budget that is already being implemented. Under special circumstances delays may be justified. The organic law (or law on the budget system) should therefore include provisions authorizing the executive to commit expenditures before the budget is approved, under specified circumstances. These provisions should be based on the budget of the previous year, rather than on a budget that has not yet been scrutinized (e.g., an authorization to commit each month up to one-twelfth of the appropriations of the previous year, as in the continuing resolution used by the U.S. Congress when the budget is not approved before the start of the fiscal year in October). In all cases, care must be taken lest these special provisions are abused and become a systematic way to sidestep the normal budget process.

Members of the legislature have different preferences regarding the manner in which resources are allocated and are subject to a variety of pressures from their constituents. The sum of these various preferences and related claims can generate a systematic tendency to increase expenditure during budget debates (a phenomenon known as "log-rolling"). Accordingly, many countries have adopted procedural rules to regulate and limit legislative debates on the budget.

These rules cover (i) the sequence of voting on the budget; and (ii) the legislature's powers to amend the budget. In parliamentary systems with a clear majority of one party, the budget prepared by the executive is routinely approved by the legislature; indeed, failure to approve the budget is equivalent to a vote of no confidence and normally results in the resignation of the government.

To enforce ex-ante fiscal discipline, in several countries the budget is voted in two phases: the overall amount of the budget is voted first, and appropriations and allocation of resources among ministries are voted only in the second phase. This procedure is aimed at protecting the aggregate expenditure limit and the overall fiscal target. The real impact of this procedure is unclear since legislators can anticipate the incidence of the overall amount of the budget on their pet programs before the first vote and decide the overall amount accordingly. However, reviewing aggregate expenditures and revenues together has the advantage of allowing the legislature to discuss macroeconomic policy explicitly.

Legal powers of the legislature to amend the budget vary from one country to another. Three situations are possible:

- *Unrestricted power* is the ability of the legislature to vary both expenditure and revenue in either direction, without the consent of the executive. Presidential systems fit this model, although the "power of the purse" granted to the legislature is counterbalanced by a presidential veto (e.g., in the U.S. and the Philippines). This implies substantial legislative influence on the first two objectives of PEM (fiscal discipline and expenditure allocation) as well as some indirect influence on the third (practical management).

- *Restricted power* is the power to amend the budget within set limits, often relating to a maximum increase in expenditures or decrease in revenues. The extent of these restricted powers varies from country to country. In the United Kingdom, France, and British Commonwealth countries, Parliaments are not allowed to propose amendments that increase expenditure and have very restricted powers. By contrast, Germany allows such amendments, but only with the consent of the executive. This implies very limited legislative influence on resource allocation and (indirectly) on operational management.
- *Balanced budget power* is the ability to raise or lower expenditures or revenues *as long as* there is a counterbalancing measure to maintain the budget balance. This intermediate arrangement concentrates legislative influence on resource allocation.

It is to be noted that limits on the power of the legislature to amend the budget are particularly needed where legislature debates lead systematically to increased expenditures, as recently the case in a number of FSU countries. The budget organic law should stipulate that legislative actions that increase expenditures can take effect only if these expenditures themselves are authorized in the budget or its supplementary acts. However, these limits should never hamper legislative review of the budget. In some countries, the budgetary role of the legislature may need to be increased rather than limited. Strong and capable committees enable the legislature to develop its expertise and play a greater role in budget decision making. Generally, different committees deal with different facets of public expenditure management.

For example, the Finance/Budget Committee reviews revenues and expenditures; a Public Accounts Committee assures legislative oversight; sectoral or standing committees deal with sectoral policy and may review sector budgets. Coordination between the activities of these committees should be effective. In countries where the role of the legislature in amending the budget is significant, amendments are prepared by committees rather than proposed on the floor by individual members.

Time allocated for the legislative budget process and, within this process, for committee reviews is important for a sound scrutiny of the budget. Legislative budget deliberations last up to 75 days in India; in the German *Bundestag* they may last up to four months; in the U.S. Congress, sometimes even longer. The legislature and its committees should have access to independent expertise for proper budget scrutiny. In India, for example, parliamentary committees are supported with secretarial functions and legislators have access to the Parliament library and associated research and reference services; the U.S. Congress benefits from competent staff of the appropriations committees as well as the services of the large and well-equipped Congressional Budget Office, and is assisted by the General Accounting Office with audits and information on program compliance and performance. Committees should also have access to administrative information. In Germany, the budget committee interacts quasi-permanently with government departments through regular departmental briefings and expenditure reports.

In India, the Public Accounts Committee receives reports and departmental accounts and revenue receipts from the Comptroller and the Auditor General (although this concerns the oversight function of the Parliament, rather than budget policies). Regular consultations between the administration and the legislative committees on budget policies and their implementation would strengthen the capacity of the legislature to review the budget.

TOWARDS REFORMS

1. Main Issues

Responsibilities of the different actors involved in budget preparation and policy formulation must be clearly defined and delimited:

- The center of government (Prime Minister, President office, etc) coordinates policy formulation and arbitrates any conflict in budget preparation.
- The Ministry of Finance prepares guidelines, scrutinizes requests and ensures the coordination of the budget preparation process, and the overall consistency of the budget with policy and macroeconomic objectives.
- Line ministries and agencies are responsible for preparing their sector programs and budgets, within the policy framework decided by the government.

Assignment of expenditures to *subnational government* should be established on clear bases, and arrangements for revenues should follow expenditure assignments. When preparing its budget, the central government should avoid passing down the deficit to subnational governments. Any increased expenditure assignment must be balanced with compensatory measures on the revenue side. To ensure both efficiency and fiscal discipline, incentives and sanctions are needed. Subnational governments should benefit from savings they make, but protective measures are required in case of mismanagement or budget overruns.

2. Directions of Reform

The legislature is the appropriate locus of overall financial accountability, and adequate means should be given to the legislature to review policies and the budget:

- The budget should be presented to the legislature in a timely manner, to allow its proper scrutiny and the completion of budgetary debates before the beginning of the fiscal year.
- Legislative committees should have adequate resources.
- Aggregate revenue, expenditure, and fiscal targets should be reviewed together.

In order to contain pressures to increase expenditures, limits on the powers of the legislature to amend the budget may be needed (e.g., any amendment that increases expenditures or decreases revenues should be accompanied by a counter24 balancing measure to maintain the initial deficit target). The legal framework should stipulate that laws that have a fiscal impact take effect only if the fiscal measures are authorized in the budget or its supplementary acts.

4

Public Finance and Public Budgeting

For understanding Budget, first we must have a look on public finance.

PUBLIC FINANCE

Public finance is a field of economics concerned with paying for collective or governmental activities, and with the administration and design of those activities. The field is often divided into questions of what the government or collective organizations should do or are doing, and questions of how to pay for those activities. The broader term, public economics, and the narrower term, government finance, are also often used.

The proper role of government provides a starting point for the analysis of public finance. In theory, under certain circumstances private markets will allocate goods and services among individuals efficiently (in the sense that no waste occurs and that individual tastes are matching with the economy's productive abilities). If private markets were able to provide efficient outcomes and if the distribution of income were socially acceptable, then there would be little or no scope for government.

In many cases, however, conditions for private market

efficiency are violated. For example, if many people can enjoy the same good at the same time (non-rival, non-excludable consumption), then private markets may supply too little of that good. National defense is one example of non-rival consumption, or of a public good. "Market failure" occurs when private markets do not allocate goods or services efficiently. The existence of market failure provides an efficiency-based rationale for collective or governmental provision of goods and services. Externalities, public goods, informational advantages, strong economies of scale, and network effects can cause market failures. Public provision via a government or a voluntary association, however, is subject to other inefficiencies, termed "government failure."

Under broad assumptions, government decisions about the efficient scope and level of activities can be efficiently separated from decisions about the design of taxation systems (Diamond-Mirlees separation). In this view, public sector programs should be designed to maximize social benefits minus costs (cost-benefit analysis), and then revenues needed to pay for those expenditures should be raised through a taxation system that creates the fewest efficiency losses caused by distortion of economic activity as possible. In practice, government budgeting or public budgeting is substantially more complicated and often results in inefficient practices. Government can pay for spending by borrowing (for example, with government bonds), although borrowing is a method of distributing tax burdens through time rather than a replacement for taxes. A deficit is the difference between government spending and revenues.

The accumulation of deficits over time is the total public debt. Deficit finance allows governments to smooth tax burdens over time, and gives governments an important fiscal policy tool. Deficits can also narrow the options of successor governments. Public finance is closely connected to issues of income distribution and social equity. Governments can reallocate income through transfer payments or by designing tax systems that treat high-income and low-income households differently.

The Public Choice approach to public finance seeks to explain how self-interested voters, politicians, and bureaucrats actually operate, rather than how they should operate.

Management

Collection of sufficient resources from the economy in an appropriate manner along with allocating and use of these resources efficiently and effectively constitute good financial management. Resource generation, resource allocation and expenditure management (resource utilization) are the essential components of a public financial management system.

Public Finance Management (PFM) basically deals with all aspects of resource mobilization and expenditure management in government. Just as managing finances is a critical function of management in any organization, similarly public finance management is an essential part of the governance process. Public finance management includes resource mobilization, prioritization of programmes, the budgetary process, efficient management of resources and exercising controls. Rising aspirations of people are placing more demands on financial resources. At the same time, the emphasis of the citizenry is on value for money, thus making public finance management increasingly vital.

Government Expenditures

Economists classify government expenditures into three main types. Government purchases of goods and services for current use are classed as government consumption. Government purchases of goods and services intended to create future benefits— such as infrastructure investment or research spending— are classed as government investment. Government expenditures that are not purchases of goods and services, and instead just represent transfers of money— such as social security payments— are called transfer payments.

Government Operations

Government operations are those activities involved in the running of a state or a functional equivalent of a state (for example, tribes, secessionist movements or revolutionary movements) for the purpose of producing value for the citizens. Government operations have the power to make, and the authority to enforce rules and laws within a civil, corporate, religious, academic, or other organization or group. In its broadest sense, "to govern" means to rule over or supervise, whether over a state, a set group of people, or a collection of people.

Income Distribution

- Income distribution - Some forms of government expenditure are specifically intended to transfer income from some groups to others. For example, governments sometimes transfer income to people that have suffered a loss due to natural disaster. Likewise, public pension programs transfer wealth from the young to the old. Other forms of government expenditure which represent purchases of goods and services also have the effect of changing the income distribution. For example, engaging in a war may transfer wealth to certain sectors of society. Public education transfers wealth to families with children in these schools. Public road construction transfers wealth from people that do not use the roads to those people that do (and to those that build the roads).

- Income Security
- Employment insurance
- Health Care

Financing of Government Expenditures

Government expenditures are financed in two ways:

- Government revenue
  - Taxes
  - Non-tax revenue (revenue from government-owned corporations, sovereign wealth funds, sales of assets, or Seigniorage
- Government borrowing

How a government chooses to finance its activities can have important effects on the distribution of income and wealth (income redistribution) and on the efficiency of markets (effect of taxes on market prices and efficiency). The issue of how taxes affect income distribution is closely related to tax incidence, which examines the distribution of tax burdens after market adjustments are taken into account. Public finance research also analyzes effects of the various types of taxes and types of borrowing as well as administrative concerns, such as tax enforcement.

Taxes

Taxation is the central part of modern public finance. Its significance arises not only from the fact that it is by far the most important of all revenues but also because of the gravity of the problems created by the present day heavy tax burden. The main objective of taxation is raising revenue. A high level of taxation is necessary in a welfare State to fulfill its obligations. Taxation is used as an instrument of attaining certain social objectives i.e. as a means of redistribution of wealth and thereby reducing inequalities. Taxation in a modern Government is thus needed not merely to raise the revenue required to meet its ever-growing expenditure on administration and social services but also to reduce the inequalities of income and wealth. Taxation is also needed to draw away money that would otherwise go into consumption and cause inflation to rise.

A tax is a financial charge or other levy imposed on an individual or a legal entity by a state or a functional equivalent of a state (for example, tribes, secessionist movements or revolutionary movements). Taxes could also be imposed by a subnational entity. Taxes consist of direct tax or indirect tax, and may be paid in money or as *corvée* labor. A tax may be defined as a "pecuniary burden laid upon individuals or property to support the government [. . .] a payment exacted by legislative authority." A tax "is not a voluntary payment or donation, but an enforced contribution, exacted pursuant to legislative authority" and is "any contribution imposed by government [. . .] whether under the name of toll, tribute, tallage, gabel, impost, duty, custom, excise, subsidy, aid, supply, or other name."

- There are various types of taxes, broadly divided into two heads - direct (which is proportional) and indirect tax (which is differential in nature):
- Stamp duty, levied on documents
- Excise tax (tax levied on production for sale, or sale, of a certain good)

- Sales tax (tax on business transactions, especially the sale of goods and services)
  - Value added tax (VAT) is a type of sales tax
  - Services taxes on specific services
- Road tax; Vehicle excise duty (UK), Registration Fee (USA), Regco (Australia), Vehicle Licensing Fee (Brazil) etc
- Gift tax
- Duties (taxes on importation, levied at customs)
- Corporate income tax on corporations (incorporated entities)
- Wealth tax
- Personal income tax (may be levied on individuals, families such as the Hindu joint family in India, unincorporated associations, etc.)

Debt

Governments, like any other legal entity, can take out loans, issue bonds and make financial investments. Government debt (also known as public debt or national debt) is money (or credit) owed by any level of government; either central or federal government, municipal government or local government. Some local governments issue bonds based on their taxing authority, such as tax increment bonds or revenue bonds.

As the government represents the people, government debt can be seen as an indirect debt of the taxpayers. Government debt can be categorized as internal debt, owed to lenders within the country, and external debt, owed to foreign lenders. Governments usually borrow by issuing securities such as government bonds and bills. Less creditworthy countries sometimes borrow directly from commercial banks or international institutions such as the International Monetary Fund or the World Bank.

Most government budgets are calculated on a cash basis, meaning that revenues are recognized when collected and outlays are recognized when paid. Some consider all government liabilities, including future pension payments and payments for goods and services the government has contracted for but not yet paid, as government debt. This approach is called accrual accounting, meaning that obligations are recognized when they are acquired, or accrued, rather than when they are paid.

Seigniorage

Seigniorage is the net revenue derived from the issuing of currency. It arises from the difference between the face value of a coin or bank note and the cost of producing, distributing and eventually retiring it from circulation. Seigniorage is an important source of revenue for some national banks, although it provides a very small proportion of revenue for advanced industrial countries.

Public Finance in Socialist Economies

Public finance in centrally planned economies has differed in fundamental ways from that in market economies. Some state-owned enterprises generated profits that helped finance government activities. The government entities that operate for profit are usually manufacturing and financial institutions, services such as nationalized healthcare do not operate for a profit to keep costs low for consumers. The Soviet Union relied heavily on turnover taxes on retail sales. Sales of natural resources, and especially petroleum products, were an important source of revenue for the Soviet Union. In Venezuela, the state-run oil company

PSDVA provides revenue for the government to fund its operations and programs that would otherwise be profit for private owners. Various market socialist systems or proposals utilize revenue generated by state-run enterprises to fund social dividends, eliminating the need for taxation altogether. In various mixed economies, the revenue generated by state-run or state-owned enterprises are used for various state endeavors; typically the revenue generated by state and government agencies goes into a sovereign wealth fund. An example of this is the Alaska Permanent Fund and Singapore's Temasek Holdings.

Statistics and Methodology

Macroeconomic data to support public finance economics are generally referred to as fiscal or government finance statistics (GFS). *The Government Finance Statistics Manual 2001 (GFSM 2001)* is the internationally accepted methodology for compiling fiscal data. It is consistent with regionally accepted methodologies such as the *European System of Accounts 1995* and consistent with the methodology of the *System of National Accounts (SNA1993)* and broadly in line with its most recent update, the *SNA2008*.

Challenges in Measuring Government

The size of governments, their institutional composition and complexity, their ability to carry out large and sophisticated operations, and their impact on the other sectors of the economy warrant a well-articulated system to measure government economic operations.

The *GFSM 2001* addresses the institutional complexity of government by defining various levels of government. The main focus of the *GFSM 2001* is the general government sector defined as the group of entities capable of implementing public policy through the provision of primarily nonmarket goods and services and the redistribution of income and wealth, with both activities supported mainly by compulsory levies on other sectors. The *GFSM 2001* disaggregates the general government into subsectors: central government, state government, and local government. The concept of general government does not include public corporations. The general government plus the public corporations comprise the public sector.

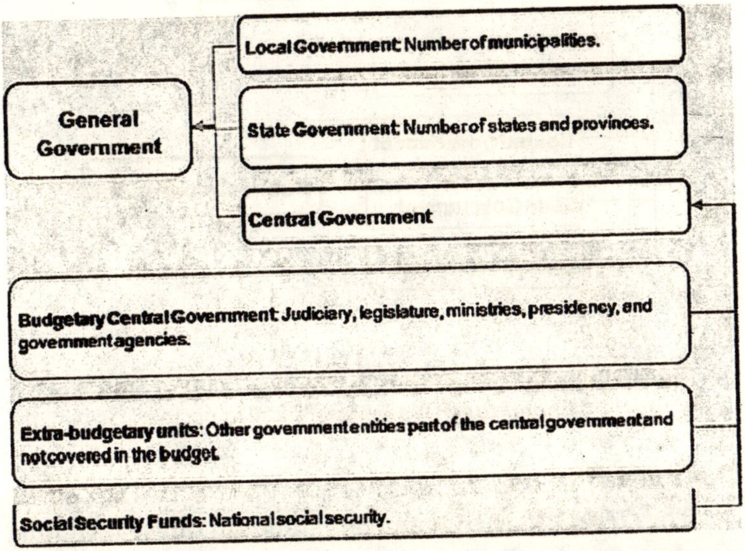

Figure 1: General Government (IMF *Government Finance Statistics Manual 2001*(Washington, 2001) pp.13

The *GFSM 2001* framework is similar to the financial accounting of businesses. For example, it recommends that governments produce a full set of financial statements including the statement of government operations (akin to the income statement), the balance sheet, and a cash flow statement. Two other similarities between the GFSM 2001 and business financial accounting are the recommended use of accrual accounting as the basis of recording and the presentations of stocks of assets and liabilities at market value. It is an improvement on the prior methodology - *Government Finance Statistics Manual 1986* – based on cash flows and without a balance sheet statement.

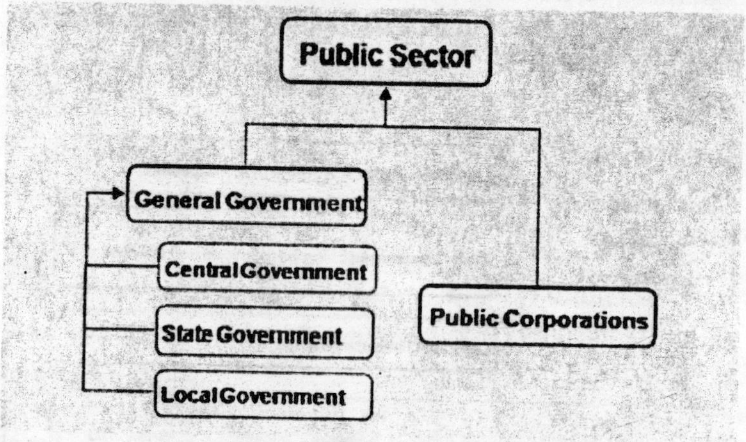

Figure 2: Public Sector(IMF *Government Finance Statistics Manual 2001*(Washington, 2001) pp.15

Users of GFS

The *GFSM 2001* recommends standard tables including standard fiscal indicators that meet a broad group of users including policy makers, researchers, and investors in sovereign debt. Government finance statistics should offer data for topics such as the fiscal architecture, the measurement of the efficiency and effectiveness of government expenditures, the economics of taxation, and the structure of public financing. The *GFSM 2001* provides a blueprint for the compilation, recording, and presentation of revenues, expenditures, stocks of assets, and stocks of liabilities. The *GFSM 2001* also defines some indicators of effectiveness in government's expenditures, for example the compensation of employees as a percentage of expense. The *GFSM 2001* includes a functional classification of expense as defined by the Classification of Functions of Government (COFOG) . This functional classification allows policy makers to analyze expenditures on categories such as health, education, social protection, and environmental protection. The financial statements can provide investors with the necessary information to assess the capacity of a government to service and repay its debt, a key element determining sovereign risk, and risk premia. Like the risk of default of a private corporation, sovereign risk is a function of the level of debt, its ratio to liquid assets, revenues and expenditures, the expected growth and volatility of these revenues and expenditures, and the cost of servicing the debt. The government's financial statements contain the relevant information for this analysis. The government's balance sheet presents the level of the debt; that is the government's liabilities. The memorandum items of the balance sheet provide additional information on the debt including its maturity and whether it is owed to domestic or external residents. The balance sheet also presents a disaggregated classification of financial and non-financial assets. These data help estimate the resources a government can potentially access to repay its debt. The statement of operations ("income statement") contains the revenue and expense accounts of the government. The revenue accounts are divided into subaccounts, including the different types of taxes, social contributions, dividends from the public sector, and royalties from natural resources. Finally, the interest expense account is one of the necessary inputs to estimate the cost of servicing the debt.

Fiscal Data Using the GFSM 2001 Methodology

GFS can be accessible through several sources. The International Monetary Fund publishes GFS in two publications: *International Financial Statistics* and the *Government Finance Statistics Yearbook*. The World Bank gathers information on external debt. On a regional level, the Organization for Economic Co-operation and Development (OECD) compiles general government account data for its members, and Eurostat, following a methodology compatible with the GFSM 2001, compiles GFS for the members of the European Union.

PUBLIC BUDGETING

Basically, Public Budgeting is a field of Public Administration and a discipline in the academic study thereof. Budgeting is characterized by its approaches, functions, formation, and type.

Robert W. Smith and Thomas D. Lynch describe public budgeting through four perspectives. The politician sees the budget process as "a political event conducted in the political arena for political advantage". The economist views budgeting as a matter of allocating resources in terms of opportunity cost where allocating resources to one consumer takes resources away from another consumer. The role of the economist, therefore, is to provide decision makers with the best possible information. The accountant perspective focuses on the accountability value in budgeting which analyzes the amount budgeted to the actual expenditures thereby describing the "wisdom of the original policy".

Some Definitions

- ***Practical:*** "A plan for financing an enterprise or government during a definite period, which is prepared and submitted by a responsible executive to a representative body (or other duly constituted agent) whose approval and authorization are necessary before the plan may be executed." ~Frederick A. Cleveland

- ***Theoretical:*** The leading question: "On what basis shall it be decided to allocate x dollars to activity A instead of activity B?" ~V. O. Key Jr.

Notable Theorists

- ***Frederick Cleveland:*** constructed a practical definition of budgeting.
- ***William F. Willoughby:*** describes the purpose of a budget document.
- ***V.O. Key, Jr.:*** sparked the normative question regarding how scarce resources ought to be distributed to unlimited demands.
- ***Verne B. Lewis:*** argued for a budgeting theory based on economic values; strongly contributing to the study of public finance.
- ***Richard A. Musgrave:*** the Father of Public Finance; identified the three roles of government in the economy: allocation of resources, distribution of goods and services, and economy stabilization.
- ***Aaron Wildavsky:*** suggested that budgetary decision making is largely political, rather than based on economic conditions.
- ***Allen Schick:*** outlined the three functions of budgeting:

  1. Strategic Planning; deciding on the goals and objectives of an organization.
  2. Management Control; management's process of

assuring effective and efficient accomplishment of goals and objectives laid out via *strategic planning*.

3. Operational Control; focused on proper execution of specific tasks that provide the most efficient and effective means of meeting the goals and objectives ordered by *management control*.

- ***Irene S. Rubin:*** facilitated the discussion of the dichotomy between theory and practice of public budgeting.

Approaches to Budgeting

A brief note on Systems Theory applied to Political Science: Inputs enter the governmental system that produces outputs which—in turn—are related to outcomes. The conversion of inputs to outputs is a measure of efficiency as the measurement of contributing inputs to impacting outcomes is a measure of efficacy.

1. *Line Item Budgeting* is arguably the simplest form of budgeting, this approach links the inputs of the system to the system. These budgets typically appear in the form of accounting documents that express minimal information regarding purpose or an explicit object within the system.
2. *Program Budgeting* takes a normative approach to budgeting in that decision making—allocating resources—is determined by the funding of one program instead of another based on what that program offers. This approach quickly lends itself to the PPBS budgeting approach.
3. *PPBS Budgeting* or—*Program Planning Budgeting System*—is the link between the line-item and

program budgets and the more complex performance budget. As opposed to the more simple program budget, this decision making tool links the program under consideration to the ways and means of facilitating the program. This is meant to serve as a long-term planning tool so that decision makers are made aware of the future implications of their actions. These are typically most useful in capital projects. The planning portion of the approach seeks to link goals to objects or expected outcomes from specific outputs, which are then sorted into programs that convert inputs to outputs; finally, the budgeting of PPBS helps determine how to fund the program. A leader in the promotion of PPBS was Robert McNamara's use in the United States Government's Department of Defense in the 1960s.

4. *Performance Based Budgeting* attempts to solve decision making problems based on a programs ability to convert inputs to outputs and/or use inputs to affect certain outcomes. Performance may be judged by a certain program's ability to meet certain objectives that contribute to a more abstract goal as calculated by that program's ability to use resources (or inputs) efficiently—by linking inputs to outputs—and/or effectively—by linking inputs to outcomes. A decision making—or allocation of scarce resources—problem is solved by determining which project maximizes efficiency and efficacy.

5. *Zero-based budgeting* is a response to an incremental decision making process whereby the budget of a given fiscal year (FY) is largely decided upon by the existing budget of FY-1. In contrast to incrementalism, the allocation of scarce resources—funding—is

determined from a zero-sum accounting method. In government, each function of a department's section proposes certain objectives that relate to some goal the section could achieve if allocated *x* dollars.

6. *Flexible Freeze* is a budgeting approach pioneered by President George H. W. Bush as a means to cut government spending. Under this approach, certain programs would be affected by changes in population growth and inflation.

7. *Program Assessment Rating Tool (P.A.R.T.)* is an instrument developed by the United States OMB to measure and assess the effectiveness of federal programs that review the program's purpose and design, strategic planning, program management, and program results and accountability. The scores are rated from effective (ranging between 85 and 100 points), moderately affective (70-84 points), adequate (50-69 points), and ineffective (0-49 points).

8. *Priority Based Budgeting* is a response to poor economic conditions. As opposed to incremental budgeting, where resource allocation is determined based on marginal shifts in costs, priority based budgeting fixes the amount of governmental resources and then allocates resources across the various programs. The programs receive their allocation based on their priority; priorities may include safe and secure communities, health, education, and community development among others. Outcome assessment then determines the efficacy of the programs. Although this approach is pro-democratic, critics suggest the administration of this process is extremely difficult.

Functions of a Budget Document

As a policy document, a government's budget is designed as a plan for implementing its policy. Traditionally, budgets served as a more rigid tool to implement policy in a retrospective setting. The functions associated with these values are listed under the Traditional Model and are control, management, and planning. With the age of information and its associated innovations, a more elastic and proactive model has emerged that is more reactive and less rigid. The Modern Model has replaced the control function with the monitoring function, the management function with the steering function, and the planning function with the strategic brokering function.

Traditional Model

Control: using the budget document to control expenditures to maximize accountability. This function is most commonly associated with line-item budgets.

Management: using the budget document to manage organizations and personnel. This function is focused on performance and efficiency. This function is most commonly associated with performance budgets.

Planning: using the budget document as a plan to achieve some goal. The focus of this function is on the outcome and effectiveness of a program. This function is most commonly associated with program and PPBS budgets.

Modern Model

Monitoring: as a response to the traditional control function, the monitoring function focuses on the *consequences* of expenditures.

Steering: as a response to the traditional management

function, the steering function serves as a *guide* for managing.

Strategic Brokering uses the budget document as a means of constantly looking for possible directions and reacting to the environment.

Values in Budgeting

Three values are generally discussed in the literature of public budgeting; accountability, efficiency, and efficacy.

Accountability focuses on the inputs going into the system or program in action and is best characterized by the Line-Item budgeting approach. It is best suited for the control and monitoring functions of a budget.

Efficiency focuses on the process of the system or program and its conversion of inputs (resources) into outputs (policy). It's focus on the process makes this value appropriate for performance budgets and most in-line with management and steering functions.

Efficacy focuses on outputs and outcomes, measuring the impact of policy. This value follows both the program budget and PPBS budget approaches and coinsides with the planning and strategic brokering functions.

Six Steps

Typically, the budget cycles occurs in four phases. The first requires policy planning and resource analysis and includes revenue estimation. The second phase is referred to as policy formulation and includes the negotiation and planning of the budget formation. The third phase is policy execution which follows budget adoption is budget execution—the implementation and revision of budgeted policy. The fourth phase encompasses the entire budget process, but is considered its fourth phase. This phase is auditing and evaluating the entire process and system. See the associated points below:

- Revenue Estimation performed in the executive branch by the finance director, clerk's office, budget director, manager, or a team.
- Budget Call issued to outline the presentation form, recommend certain goals.
- Budget Formulation reflecting on the past, set goals for the future and reconcile the difference.
- Budget Hearings can include departments, sections, the executive, and the public to discuss changes in the budget.
- Budget Adoption final approval by the legislative body.
- Budget Execution amending the budget as the fiscal year progresses.

Types of Public Budgets

- Operating budgets are those documents that describe the expenditures and revenues during a given period for the functioning of an organization.
- Capital budgeting is the process of planning for future purchases above a certain cost threshold or extended life span. This budget is typically accompanied by a Capital Improvement Plan that describes a timeline for acquisition and payment of debt.

REFERENCES

Anthony B. Atkinson and Joseph E. Stiglitz (1980). *Lectures in Public Economics*, McGraw-Hill Economics Handbook Series

Cleveland, Frederick A.(1915)"Evolution of the Budget Idea in the United States". *The Annals of the American Academy of Political and Social Science*. 15-35.

Columbia Encyclopedia, *Government*, Columbia University Press.

James M. Buchanan and Richard A. Musgrave (1989). *Public Finance and Public Choice: Two Contrasting Visions of the State*. MIT Press

Joseph E. Stiglitz (2000). *Economics of the Public Sector*, 3rd ed. Norton.

Key Jr., V. O.(1940)*American Political Science Review* 34. 1137-40.

Lewis, Verne E. (Winter 1952) *Public Administration Review* 12.1. 43-54.

R.A. Musgrave (1987). "public finance," *The New Palgrave: A Dictionary of Economics*, v. 3, pp. 1055–60.

Richard A. Musgrave (1959). *The Theory of Public Finance: A Study in Political Economy*.

Richard A. Musgrave and Peggy B. Musgrave (1973). *Public Finance in Theory and Practice*

Robert Barro and Vittorio Grilli (1994), *European Macroeconomics*, Ch. 15-16. Macmillan.

Rubin, Irene S. (1990) "Budget Theory and Budget Practice: How Good the Fit?" *Public Administration Review* March/April 1990. 179-89.

Rubin, Irene S. (1997) *The Politics of Public Budgeting: Getting and Spending, Borrowing and Balancing*. Third Edition, Chatham House Publishers: Chatham, New Jersey.

Schick, Allen. (December 1966) *Public Administration Review* 26. 243-58.

Smith, Robert W. and Thomas D. Lynch. (2004) *Public Budgeting in America*. 5th Edition. Pearson;Upper Saddle River,. New Jersery. 37.

Walsh, Mary Williams. "Richard A. Musgrave, 96, Theoretician of Public Finance, Dies". January 20, 2007. New York Times: Business.

Wildavsky, Aaron. (Autumn 1961) *Public Administration Review* 21. 183-190.

Willoughby, William F. (1918) "The Movement for Budgetary Reform in the States". *D. Appleton and Company for the Institute for Government Research*. 1-8.

5

Budgeting and Accounting in India

India is a Union of States and Union Territories. The responsibilities and powers (including financial) of the Union and the States, and the relationship between them, are set out in the Constitution of India. The legislative powers are detailed in three lists-Union, State and Concurrent. The Union list includes matters of national interest such as foreign affairs, railways, posts and telegraphs, currency and coinage, and inter-state trade and commerce while the State list contains matters of regional interest such as law and order, health, agriculture, irrigation, power, rural and community development. Certain matters of common interest, such as economic and social planning, have been placed under the concurrent legislative powers of the Union and the States. In the event of a clash between the laws of the Union and the States in the concurrent area, the laws of the former prevail.

In fact, the, Constitution of India allots separate legislative heads of taxation to the Union and the States. Borrowing and foreign exchange entitlements are controlled by the Union. The residual powers of levying taxes not mentioned in the State list and the Concurrent list also rest with the Union. The division of fields of taxation between the Union and the States is based on economic and administrative rationale. The power to levy taxes with an inter-state base, and where uniformity in rates is desirable, is vested in the Union Government, but the power to levy taxes that are location- specific lies with the States. However, certain taxes are levied by the Union but are collected and retained by the States, while certain other taxes and duties are levied and collected by the Union but their net proceeds are assigned to or shared with the States. The Constitution provides for payment by the Union of grants-in-aid of revenues to the States. The Government of India is also empowered to make loans to the States or give guarantees in respect of loans raised by them. There is also provision for grants by the Union or a State for any public purpose.

The audit of the accounts of the Union and of the States is a Union responsibility. Accordingly the accounts of the Union and of the States are to be kept in such form as the President of India prescribes on the advice of the Comptroller and Auditor General of India (CAG). There is thus a unified system of auditing and accounting, facilitated by Parliament enacting a law governing the duties, powers and conditions of service of the CAG known as the Comptroller and Auditor General's (Duties, Powers and Conditions of Service) Act 1971.

The financial management systems and accountability mechanisms, both at Union and State levels, are almost the same except in certain details. Unless specifically mentioned, the systems detailed below in respect of the Union apply also to the States.

Financial Procedure

Basically, the executive authority of the Union is vested in the President of India who exercises this authority either directly or through officers in accordance with constitutional provisions. However the President has been placed under a firm constitutional obligation to act in accordance with the advice tendered by the Council of Ministers headed by the Prime Minister. In the States it is the Governor who discharges the executive functions of the State with the aid and advice of the Council of Ministers headed by the Chief Minister. The financial year in India is from 1 April to the 31 March of the following year. The annual financial statement of receipts and expenditure of the Government is required to be placed before the Parliament/State Legislature which, in each case, confers specific authority for raising revenue through taxation and incurring expenditure. In this regard, no tax can be levied or collected except by authority of law while, similarly, no moneys can be appropriated from the Consolidated Fund except in accordance with law and for the purposes and in the manner provided in the Constitution.

Constitution of Funds

The Constitution of India provides for the creation of three separate funds both at the Union and State levels.

(a) **Constituted Funds:** All revenues received by a Government, all loans raised by that Government by the issue of treasury bills, loans or ways and means advances and all moneys received by that Government in repayment of loans, form the one Consolidated Fund.

(b) **Constingency Funds:** The Contingency Fund is in the nature of an imprest, into which are paid from time to time such sums of money as may be determined by law. The Fund is placed at the disposal of the President of India or the Governor of the State, as the case may be, to enable advances to be made for the purpose of meeting unforeseen expenditure pending authorisation of such expenditure by Parliament or State Legislature.

(c) **Public Account:** All other moneys not forming part of the Consolidated Fund, received by or on behalf of the Government, are credited to the Public Account.

The demarcation of moneys received by the Union or a State Government into three separate funds is based on a rational basis. All the moneys whether received by way of tax or non-tax revenues, or from any other source where the ownership of the moneys vests with the Government, form part of the Consolidated Fund. Moneys received by or on behalf of the Government where the Government acts as a trustee form part of the Public Account. The nature of the Contingency Fund is self-evident. No moneys can be withdrawn from the Consolidated Fund for incurring any expenditure without prior approval of the Parliament or the State Legislature through a process of legal appropriation. Therefore unforeseen expenditures, or expenditure in excess of approved appropriations, are met from the Contingency Fund. The Parliament of India and the various State Legislatures have passed laws establishing such Contingency Funds.

Parliament and Financial Accountability and Management

Although the Indian Constitution does not mention the term 'Budget', it provides that the President shall in respect of every financial year cause to be laid before both the Houses (The Houses are the House of the People (Lok Sabha) and the Council of States (Rajya Sabha)) of Parliament a statement of the estimated receipts and expenditure of the Government of India for that year. This statement, known as the Annual Financial Statement, is the main fiscal or budgetary document of the Government.

The estimates of expenditure embodied in the Annual Financial Statement are required to show separately :

(a) Sums required to meet expenditure described under the Constitution as 'Charged' upon the Consolidated Fund of India.

(b) Sums required to meet other expenditure proposed to be made from this Fund, i.e., expenditure which is subject to Vote of the Parliament.

The estimates are also required to distinguish expenditure on revenue account from that on capital account. A further classification of expenditure is made on the basis of its being a part of 'Plan Outlay' or non-plan, i.e. expenditure which is part of normal governmental activities or maintenance expenditure.

The expenditure of the following nature is charged on the Consolidated Fund and is not subject to Vote of Parliament:

i) emoluments and other allowances of the President of India; Presiding Officers of the two Houses of Parliament;

ii) salaries and allowances, etc. of the Judges of the Supreme Court; Comptroller and Auditor General of India;

iii) debt redemption charges, including interest;

iv) any sums required to satisfy any judgment of the Court or a legal tribunal, as also

v) any other expenditure which might be declared by the Parliament by law to be a charged expenditure.

The expenditure estimates which form part of the Annual Financial Statement are divided into different Demands for Grants. The Demands for Grants, as mentioned earlier, show separately the revenue and capital, and the charged and voted expenditure. Similarly, estimates of receipts are classified in the tax and non-tax categories and also those which are on revenue account and others which are on capital account (in common with public loans). The Demands for Grants (voted portion) are submitted before the Lok Sabha and put to vote.

This House has the power to assent or refuse to assent or reduce the amount of the Demand. The Demands relating to 'Charged' expenditure are not subject to any vote, but Parliament is free to discuss any of these Demands and express its opinion for the consideration of the Government. The Demands for Grants before they are submitted to the Parliament require a specific recommendation of the President (or Governor in the case of a State).

After the Demands for Grants have been approved by the Lok Sabha (or the State Legislative Assembly), an Appropriation Bill to authorise the Government to withdraw moneys from the Consolidated Fund is required to be introduced and passed by the Parliament (or the State Legislature). It is through the medium of this Appropriation Act that the constitutional requirement of parliamentary financial control is met. A similar procedure is mandatory for providing supplementary or additional funds required in a particular financial year, and for regularising any excess expenditure over the approved appropriations. For this purpose, Supplementary Demands for Grants or Demands for Excess Grants have to be presented and relevant Appropriation Acts passed.

Votes on Account

Since India has an annual budget cycle in respect of each Appropriation, the entire budgetary process is to be completed, according to constitutional and legal requirements, for the next financial year, before the end of the current financial year i.e. before 31 March. In a country of the size of India with widespread activities of the Government, the budgetary process has to start at least six to seven months before the commencement of the next financial year. The process of estimation starting from the lowest activity centre up to the apex level of the Ministry of Finance and the Cabinet has to be completed at least a month before the commencement of the next financial year. Therefore, normally by end of February, the budget estimates and other related documents are presented to the Parliament. It is, however, not possible always to complete the entire legal process of consideration, discussion and approval of the estimates and related appropriation and other finance bills before 31 March. In order therefore to enable the Executive to carry on the activities of the Government uninterruptedly, the mechanism of allowing supplies in the interim for a part of the financial year has been provided through the medium of Vote on Account.

The Executive and Financial Accountability and Management

The Council of Ministers headed by the Prime Minister is collectively responsible to the Parliament. Each Minister holding a portfolio for formulating departmental policies is individually responsible (as part of that collective responsibility) to oversee the implementation and ensure the efficient working of the administrative machinery under his charge.

Individual Ministers are responsible to the legislature for actions of their respective civil servants, who, in turn, are ministerially accountable. Accountability is made more specific and is ensured by a complex set of organisational and procedural devices.

Ministry of Finance

The control over finances of Government has traditionally been confined to the Ministry of Finance. With the phenomenal growth and the complexity of Government activities, several powers have been delegated to Administrative Ministries, but the Ministry of Finance continues to have the overall responsibility of co-ordination and control. For speedy and effective discharge of their functions in financial matters which include planning, programming, budgeting, internal control, monitoring and evaluation, an Integrated Financial Adviser is attached to each Administrative Ministry. The Integrated Financial Adviser acts both as internal and external financial adviser. He functions as internal financial adviser in the exercise of powers delegated to the Ministries under the Delegation of Financial Power Rules, and acts as an external financial adviser on behalf of the Ministry of Finance in respect of matters outside the delegated financial powers of the Administrative Ministry.

The Ministry of Finance has issued detailed regulations on financial management and control to be followed uniformly in the Government of India. In addition, the Ministry is responsible for framing rules relating to the maintenance of accounts of the Union and of the States, on the advice of the CAG.

Administrative Ministries

The basic responsibility for the administration of each department's activities is entrusted to the Head of the department concerned, who is guided and controlled by the Administrative Ministry. In financial matters each head of the department is thus responsible for the collection of revenue and control of expenditure pertaining to his department, the receipt and disbursement of which are usually effected at various places and through various persons. The Ministries also exercise financial control over public enterprises set up under each of them. The Permanent Secretary of each Ministry who is the Chief Accounting Authority for that Ministry, discharges this function through and with the assistance of the Controller of Accounts and the Financial Adviser.

Once the Appropriation Bill (Vote on Account) or the Appropriation Bill relating to the whole year, as the case may be, is passed by Parliament, the Ministry of Finance advises the other Administrative Ministries of the Grants made by the Lok Sabha and the Appropriations sanctioned by Parliament. Each Ministry of the Union Government may distribute the funds, where necessary, among the controlling and disbursing officers subordinate to it. Unspent balances are unavailable for utilisation in the following year. Officers incurring or authorising expenditure from public moneys must comply with the prescribed standards of financial propriety.

The various Ministries are responsible for the control of expenditure against the financial grants and appropriations placed at their disposal, control being exercised through the respective Controlling Officers. For this purpose there are well laid down procedures and management information systems. All anticipated savings in the grants are surrendered to the Ministry of Finance, before the close of the financial year, for possible reappropriation as permissible under the rules of appropriation.

Transfer of Appropriation

No expenditure can be incurred which may have the effect of exceeding a grant authorised by law for a financial year, except after obtaining a supplementary grant or an advance from the Contingency Fund. Since voted and charged portions-in common with the revenue and capital sections of individual grants-are distinct and reappropriation inter se is not permissible, an excess in any one portion or section is treated as an excess in that particular grant. However, reappropration of funds from one primary unit of appropriation to another such unit within a grant may be sanctioned by a competent authority at any time before the close of the financial year, subject to certain restrictions.

Other Central Agencies

Besides the Ministry of Finance, the Finance Commission and the Planning Commission play an important role in public finances of the country. The Finance Commission makes recommendations relating to the distribution of net proceeds of certain taxes between the Union and the States and the payment of grants-in-aid of the revenues of the States out of the Consolidated Fund of India. The Planning Commission, besides formulating and monitoring development plans, advises the Union Government regarding the desirable transfer to the States of resources essential for developmental outlays. These transfers are over and above those recommended by the Finance Commission. Its recommendations cover among other things, feasible changes in tax rates and efforts, quantum and allocation of borrowings between the Union and the States.

The Reserve Bank of India (RBI)

It is remarkable that as the Apex financial institution, Reserve Bank of India, which has been set up as a Central Bank by an Act of Parliament is the repository of all cash balances of the Government of India and of all the States except in the case of two States. It plays a vital role in assisting the Government in the economic management of the country, particularly the monetary system. The Government of India borrows from the Reserve Bank against issue of treasury bills for replenishing its cash balance from time to time. The State governments also obtain ways and means advances as bridging loans from the Bank which are repayable within a specified period.

The Reserve Bank has been entrusted with the responsibility of management of public debt raised by the Government of India and of the States including maintenance of detailed accounts of all the loans floated. The Bank has also been entrusted with the complete control of foreign exchange of the country.

Privatisation

In India there has been a growing awareness among the public sector policy makers and executives of public enterprises of the need to take various remedial measures to correct adverse trends in public enterprises. There is a quest for increasing efficiency, optimising performance and ensuring better financial results. With the exception of a few small public enterprises which have been wound up, there has been no concrete case of 'privatisation' in India, as it is commonly understood. However the Government of India has recently sold limited shares of some public enterprises to mutual funds and has announced its intention of selling up to 49 percent of equity to certain financial institutions and to the public.

The Supreme Audit Institution (SAI)

The Comptroller and Auditor General of India (CAG) plays a crucial role in parliamentary financial control. The Indian Constitution provides for a unitary and independent audit by the CAG. The audited Appropriation and Finance Accounts are submitted along with the audit reports of the CAG to the President of India or the Governors of the States according to whether they relate to the Union or the States. These accounts and reports are then caused to be laid before the Union Parliament or the State Legislatures concerned.

The primary function of the audit of the CAG is to verify the accounts to ascertain (1) whether the moneys shown in the accounts as having been disbursed were legally available for and applicable to the service or purpose to which they have been applied or charged and whether the expenditure conforms to the authority which governs it and (2) whether the assessment, collection and allocation of revenue have been properly done. The Appropriation and Finance Accounts are accordingly examined under the directions of the CAG and certified as to their correctness subject to his observations in his Reports on the Accounts submitted under Article 151 of the Constitution.

The jurisdiction of the CAG extends to the audit of Government commercial enterprises, as well as to bodies and authorities substantially financed from Government revenues. The CAG also examines the accounts relating to grants and loans given by the Government to other bodies. There is also an enabling provision in the Act passed by the Union Parliament in 1971 to take up the audit of any other bodies or authorities with the approval of, or at the request of, the President or the Governors as the case may be.

The CAG has the authority to make regulations on the scope of audit. Such regulations are not subject to the approval of either the Government of the day or the Parliament. Thus, the CAG has complete discretion to regulate the scope of his audit. Apart from the traditional forms of audit, commonly known as the appropriation audit and regularity audit, the discretionary forms of audit (the propriety audit and the efficiency-cum-performance audit) developed by the CAG have assumed significance from the viewpoint of 'accountability' in a comprehensive sense. The audit looks beyond the mere regularity of expenditure to its prudence and economy and to a general examination of the efficiency and effectiveness with which an organisation is discharging its financial responsibilities.

The powers of the CAG to have access to documents and information in connection with audit of accounts have been enhanced under the Act of 1971. Earlier, in certain cases he was obliged to accept a simple statement of facts derived from a book or document which the highest executive authority certified as secret. Now, no such restriction exists and the CAG can call for any document as long as it is considered relevant to the transactions to which his auditing duties extend. Further, the Act specifically enjoins that the administration shall afford all facilities for his inspection and comply with his request for information in as complete a form as possible and with all reasonable expedition.

Relationship with Parliamentary Committee

The audit reports of the CAG, other than those relating to commercial enterprises, are considered by the Public Accounts Committees. The Committees on Public Undertakings consider the audit reports relating to commercial enterprises. The various committees examine the many audit reports on a selective basis, assisted by the

CAG or his Principal Audit Officers as follows:

- Assistance in the selection of subjects.
- Supply of background information and memorandum of important points.
- Briefing of the working groups/sub-committees for a proper undertstanding of the subject.
- Briefing of the chairmen of the committees, as and when necessary.
- Attendance at the sittings of the committees to assist in their examination of witnesses.
- Vetting of written submissions of the witnesses for ensuring factual accuracy.
- Factual verification of the reports of the committees.
- Assistance at the sittings of the committees devoted to deliberation on and adoption of their reports.
- Vetting of the notes of government on action taken on the committees' recommendations.
- factual verification of the follow-up reports of the committees.
- Attendance to assist the committees at the sittings for consideration and adoption of their follow-up reports.

Informal assistance is also given to the individual members and the secretariat of the committees so as to enable them to have a proper understanding of the issues dealt with in the relevant audit report. In India the audit reports as such are not generally discussed in the Parliament or State Legislatures. However the recommendations of the committees are by convention considered as the recommendations of the entire Parliament.

Hence, the assistance given by the CAG and his office to the Financial Committees is in effect assistance to the entire legislature. Even in regard to those issues dealt with in the audit reports which have not been taken up by the committees for detailed oral or other examination, notes on remedial action taken by individual departments of government are required to be submitted to the committees, after the notes are vetted by the Audit Department. The Public Undertakings Committee of Parliament, besides considering some of the reports of Comptroller and Auditor General, carries out its own examination of the working of a number of public commercial enterprises. There is a need here for closer coordination between the CAG and the Committee in selection of the subjects for audit appraisals of public undertakings to avoid duplication of efforts.

Auditing Standards

As pointed out earlier, the CAG has full authority to determine the scope and extent of his audit. The auditing standards followed in India have evolved over many years during which state audit has been practised in this country. These auditing standards have been incorporated in various manuals issued by the CAG for the guidance of his officers. Specific criteria and procedures of audit have also been laid down in separate manuals on various audit disciplines.

In the audit of the financial statements of commercial departments of the government or of the many public enterprises, Generally Accepted Auditing Standards (GAAS) as applicable to comparable enterprises in private sector are observed. The CAG has, however, the right to issue directions to the professional accountants who conduct the primary audit of public sector companies, indicating to them the manner in which the audit of such enterprises is to be conducted. The CAG also reviews the performance of such auditors.

Other Parliamentary Committees

Estimates Committee

In addition to the financial surveillance of the Public Accounts Committee and the Committee on Public Undertakings, the Estimates Committee examines the estimates of the Governments to determine the financial propriety of planned revenues and expenditures, subject to policy constraints. The Estimates Committee subsequently reports on any economies, improvements in systems, or reforms, which may be effected. Where necessary, alternative policies to achieve increased efficiency and economy in administration are suggested. It is also one of the functions of this Committee to recommend the form in which the budget estimates are to be presented to Parliament.

Subject Committees

Other parliamentary committees have been established recently for the specialised examination of government activities in such fields as agriculture, environment and forest, and science and technology. Although these specialised committees and the Estimates Committee may utilise the information contained in the various audit reports of the CAG, so far there has been no established convention of the CAG assisting them in their examination and reporting activities.

Budgeting System

Developmental Plans and Budget

The traditional budget is generally an incremental line-item budget based on historical or empirical methods of estimating revenues and expenditures. Soon after national independence, the Government launched comprehensive socio-economic development through five year plans, divided into annual plans. Apart from a detailed planning process, these involved three major concerns:

(a) raising and allocating additional resources-both internal and external;

(b) enlarging the responsibility functions of budgets, and

(c) strengthening the systems of expenditure control.

Programme and Performance Budgeting

Following national independence, there was a growing awareness by legislators, taxpayers and budget authorities of the need for a structural change in the budget so that additional budgetary input could be compared with additional output. In 1965 the United Nations published a Manual for Programme and Performance Budgeting and suggested that the developing countries could adopt this technique with the view to obtaining a better return on resources. The Indian Government appointed a high-level Administrative Reforms Commission which recommended the introduction of a performance budget as an instrument for budgeting in terms of physical inputs and outputs, in addition to budgeting purely on financial terms.

As a result of this recommendation performance budgets were developed taking into account international practices in conjunction with the national planning structure. The Planning Commission, which acts as the apex body of planning in India for all sectors, substantially performs the planning functions of the budget, in contrast to other countries where these are handled by the Ministry of Finance, the Treasury or other budgetary authorities. Performance budgets in India are prepared in addition to the budgetary documents required under constitutional or other legal provisions. Emphasis is placed on comparing the effects of financial inputs with physical outputs. These budgets provide various performance indicators in both financial and physical terms.

Zero-Base Budgeting

Following a considerable period of investigation and examination, zero-base budgeting was adopted in India in 1986 as a technique for determining expenditure budgets. Accordingly the Ministry of Finance instructed all the administrative ministries to review their respective programmes and activities in order to prepare expenditure budget estimates based on the principles of zero-base budgeting. Although this budgeting system has not yet been fully implemented in India, it is envisaged that the following essential steps should be taken by all ministries and departments:

(i) Establishment of precise objectives for each function, and programme or project;

(ii) Identification and analysis of decision units;

(iii) Formulation of decision packages; and

(iv) Ranking of decision packages.

There has been some resistance by ministries and departments to the full implementation of zero-base budgeting. However a much more stringent degree of scrutiny and cost benefit analysis with clear prioritization of activities and programmes will have to be done if budgetary imbalances are not to be allowed to go beyond control.

Budget Classification

The estimates of receipts are made under three main divisions viz. Revenue Receipts (all direct and indirect taxes, non-tax receipts and interest on loans and advances); Capital Receipts (internal debt, external debt and repayment of loans and advances) and Public Account (debt other than that falling under Capital Receipts, deposits, advances, etc.).

The estimates of expenditure from the Consolidated Fund fall into two categories-Non-plan expenditure and Plan expenditure. Each comprises expenditure on revenue account and on capital account, including loans and advances separately.

Budget Planning and Budget Steps

Planning

The Government of India has constituted a body known as the Planning Commission with the Prime Minister as its Chairman and members comprising eminent personalities from the various fields of economics, agriculture, education, industry, social sciences and public administration. Socio-economic development planning attempted by the Commission covers the entire country including the States. Nationwide coordination is obtained through the National Development Council represented by the Chief Ministers of all the States. The planning process takes into account (i) the required growth rate of the Gross Domestic Product (GDP), (ii) the growth rates for various sectors of economy, (iii) the sources of funding, and (iv) the methodology of achieving the planned goals. The Planning Commission also examines and gives its expert advice on various projects and programmes.

The five year plans are formulated and are then de-segregated into annual plans. The annual plans are then prepared in respect of each sector. These are further demarcated between the Union Government and States. Thereafter, the process of entrustment to various ministries and departments takes place. The orientation of the budgets in India is largely determined by plan outlays, their composition and sources of funding.

Organisation for Budget Management

The Finance Minister, assisted inter alia by the Budget Division of the Department of Economic Affairs of the Ministry of Finance, has responsibility for producing the budget, in the form of the Annual Financial Statement and such supplementary budgets as may be needed during a year for the Government of India (other than for the railways). The Budget Division is responsible for issuing all instructions and guidelines for the preparation of budget estimates and for monitoring the timely receipt of the same from all the Ministries concerned. The railway budget is prepared separately and presented to the Parliament a few days in advance of the general budget. The railway budget figures (net) are, however, also incorporated in the general budget to give an overall picture of the financial position. The Railway Budget is presented to Parliament by the Minister of Railways.

Budget Steps

The General Financial Rules prescribe the broad guidelines, procedures and forms for the preparation of budget estimates of receipts and expenditure by the ministries. In addition, the Budget Division issues a circular, normally during September each year, known as the 'Budget Circular1 for the next financial year (which is 1 April to 31 March as indicated earlier) for preparation of the Revised Estimates of the current financial year and the budget estimates of the ensuing financial year. This circular gives detailed instructions about the preparation of estimates of receipts and expenditure, the required format and the various statements that are to be appended to the estimates. It also specifies the processes to be followed and their scheduled dates.

The estimating authorities prepare the detailed estimates of receipts separately for each Major Head of account. For each Major Head, break-up of minor/detailed heads (to be in conformity with the accounting classification) is given, taking into account the actuals for the past three years. Relevant notes are given to highlight any individual items of significance or explanation for any major variation with reference to past actuals. The detailed estimates of expenditure are prepared by the estimating authorities by each unit of appropriation (sub/detailed head) under the prescribed Major and Minor Heads of Account separately for Plan and Non-plan expenditure. The estimates of Plan expenditure are made on the basis of the approved plan allocations intimated by the Planning Commission.

The estimating authorities forward the budget proposals to their departmental heads for consideration and onward transmission to the ministries administratively concerned. These ministries scrutinise the estimates, make modifications where necessary, and transmit these revised estimates to the Financial Adviser for further examination and processing. The Financial Adviser ensures the correctness of accounts classification, makes modifications as may be called for in his judgement in the context of economy and other considerations, consolidates the estimates for each programme/organisation to present a complete picture of their financial costs, and obtains approval of the Secretary (Expenditure) in the Ministry of Finance, wherever necessary. Departmental budgets are then forwarded to the Budget Division. While the prescribed date for receipt of the estimates of receipts by the Budget Division is normally not later than the end of December, the date for estimates of expenditure is 31 October. The estimates of departmental receipts and expenditure received in the Budget Division are duly scrutinised and then accepted for incorporation in the Budget.

The CAG provides the Union and State Governments with any information requested from time to time regarding accounts for the compilation and maintenance of which he is responsible. The CAG also renders all reasonable assistance sought by the respective Governments in the preparation of their annual financial statements (budget estimates).

Before finalising the budget proposals the Finance Minister holds informal meetings with organisations representing industry, agriculture and other key sectors. He also meets leading economists to ascertain their views on matters having a bearing on the fiscal policies of the Government. The budget proposals are placed before the Parliament by the end of February. The railway budget, as already mentioned, is presented separately a few days in advance of the general budget.

Public Debt

The task of finding sufficient resources to fund plan outlays has become exceedingly difficult. Additionally, in common with most developing countries, India has also had to face the impact of several adverse global economic and fiscal developments. Unavoidably there has been the need to import a necessary minimum of raw materials, machinery, equipment and even technology. Such imports have considerably strained the foreign exchange resources of the country. In view of the above problems, India, in common with many other countries, has had to resort to large scale borrowings both from the domestic economy and through international sources.

The Constitution of India empowers the Union and State Governments to borrow under certain conditions and within certain limits. The Government of India can borrow upon the security of the Consolidiated Fund of India within such limits as may be fixed by law by the Parliament from time to time. A State Government can borrow only within the country upon the security of the Consolidiated Fund of the State within such limits as may be fixed by the Legislature of the State. The consent of the Government of India is necessary for raising a fresh loan in case the Union government has already guaranteed an outstanding loan of the State or if the State owes a debt to the Union Government.

Domestic Borrowings: Following are the main sources of borrowings by the Government of India :

(i) Raising of public loans.

(ii) Use of fiscal instruments such as Treasury Bills.

(iii) Borrowings from financial institutions.

(iv) Obtaining credit through the Central Bank of India.

In addition, India has a very large network of voluntary schemes for promoting savings by individual investors. Known as National Savings Schemes, these have contributed substantial amounts to the resources needed by the Government.

The public sector enterprises have also been allowed to negotiate public borrowings through the medium of bonds, public deposits, and other financial instruments. These may be required to be guaranteed by the Government.

External Debt: Following are the main sources of borrowings by the Government of India for meeting foreign exchange requirements :

(i) Loans from multi-lateral agencies such as the International Bank of Reconstruction and Development (IBRD) and the International Monetary Fund (IMF).

(ii) Bilateral arrangements for loan assistance.

(iii) Suppliers credit, i.e. equipment and machinery imported on deferred payment basis.

(iv) Assistance through commodity and technology import.

(v) Borrowing on commercial terms, mostly through public sector undertakings.

Some financial assistance is also available as an outright grant, or at a very nominal interest rate, or as a long term deferred credit. However most of the financial assistance comprises loans with varying terms regarding the repayment period and interest rates.

The major phenomenon of public debt in India has been its increasing size and cost in terms of interest burden. Similarly, the large liability for external payments and other related factors have caused a severe strain on the external value of Indian currency. Although the Constitution provides for limits on borrowings, the Government has so far not acted on this provision.

Budget Documents

Besides the Annual Financial Statement and the Demands for Grants, the following documents are also presented to Parliament as part of the overall budget:

1. 'Economic Survey' : This gives a background to the economic trends prevailing in the country. It also gives an analysis of the agricultural and industrial production, money supply, imports and exports and other relevant factors which have a bearing on the framing of the budget so that the Parliament may have a better appreciation of the efforts made by the Government for mobilising resources and their allocation in terms of development priorities.
2. 'Public Enterprises Survey' : This contains a detailed report on the operations of commercial public enterprises. Besides, the reports of the Comptroller and Auditor General of India on the operation of various public sector enterprises are also presented to Parliament during the budget session.
3. 'Expenditure Budgets' : This gives not only the estimates in terms of revenue and capital under Plan and Non-plan heads in relation to each administrative unit, but also a description of expenditure in terms of major programmes. These are distinct from and in addition to 'Demands for Grants'.
4. 'Receipts Budget' : Estimates of receipts included in the Annual Financial Statement are further analysed in this document. The document also gives details of revenue and capital receipts, the trend of receipts over the years and, more importantly the details of external assistance received by the Government.

5. 'Performance Budgets' : These budgets are prepared by all ministries dealing with development activities. Also provided are separate appraisal reports in respect of certain major Central Sector Projects/ Programmes. A statement is included on the programmes and performances of each public sector undertaking under the respective administrative ministry, indicating the installed and utilised capacity, physical targets and achievements, results of operations, and return on capital.

6. 'Budget at a Glance' : This document provides information regarding the total expenditure and resources, both for meeting Plan Outlays as well as under the scheme of devolution of financial resources envisaged in the Constitution, transferred from Union budget to the budgets of State Governments.

7. Following the budget speech of the Finance Minister (which is also printed in two volumes and placed before the Parliament along with the budget documents), a Finance Bill is introduced incorporating the fiscal proposals of the Government for the levy of new taxes, modification of the existing tax structure or continuance of the existing tax structure beyond a period approved by the Parliament.

8. To facilitate understanding of the taxation proposals contained in the Finance Bill, the provisions of the Bills are explained in simple language in a separate document called 'Memorandum Explaining the Provisions of the Finance Bill'.

Later in the budgetary process, the Ministry of Finance produces a document known as 'The Economic and Functional Classification of the Central Government Budget'. This

BUDGET PROCESS

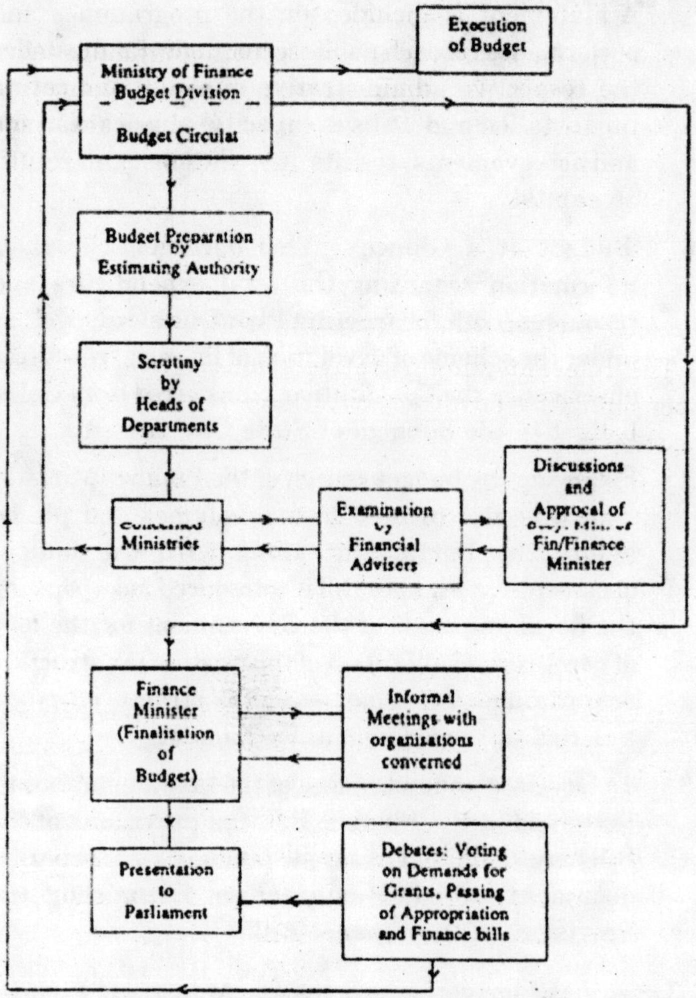

gives an appreciation of the impact of Government receipts and expenditure on the other sectors of the economy by regrouping the budgetary aggregates in terms of economic magnitudes-for example, the amount spent on capital formation directly by the Government and transferred to other sectors of economy.

The discussions relating to the annual budget in Parliament take place in two stages. In the first stage general discussions centre around the budget speech of the Finance Minister. In the second stage, detailed discussions take place on the 'Demands for Grants'.

Budget Implementation

Role of Departments in Spending and Control

The relevant administrative ministry has the main responsibility for ensuring that (i) expenditure is incurred for the approved purpose, (ii) it is within the sums allotted, (iii) it has been incurred under the authority competent to sanction it, and (iv) due prudence has been shown in its incurrence. As ministries have delegated their powers to lower functionaries, the basic responsibility is shifted to the particular functionary concerned, but overall responsibility remains with the administrative ministry.

As per rules, no public authority can incur any expenditure or enter into any liability involving expenditure or transfer of moneys for investment or deposit from government account unless such expenditure or transfer, as the case may be has been sanctioned by general or special orders of the Government or by any authority to which power has been delegated in this reagard. No expenditure can be incurred against a sanction unless funds are made available to meet the expenditure by valid appropriation or reappropriation. The government authorities have to comply with rules prescribed in the General Financial Rules and the Delegation of Financial Power Rules in all financial matters. The designated controlling authorities have to ensure not only that the total expenditure is kept within the limits of the authorised grants but also that the funds allotted to spending units are expended in the public interest and on objects for which the money was provided.

In order to maintain proper control, the controlling officer obtains information on not only what has actually been spent from the grants but also what commitments and liabilities have been and will be incurred against them. He must be in a position to assume, before the Government and Public Accounts Committee, complete responsibility for departmental expenditure and to explain or to justify any instance of excess expenditure or financial irregularity that may be brought to notice as a result of audit scrutiny or otherwise. In the discharge of his ultimate responsibility for the administration of a grant, or a part thereof, placed at his disposal, every controlling officer must satisfy himself not only that adequate provisions exist within the departmental organisation for systematic internal checks calculated to prevent and detect errors and irregularities in the financial proceedings of his subordinate officers and to guard against waste and loss of public money and stores, but also that the prescribed checks are effectively applied. As regards receipts, it is the duty of the departments concerned to ensure that the dues of Government are correctly and promptly assessed and paid into the treasury/bank. All moneys received by or on behalf of Government either as dues of Government or for deposit, remittance or otherwise are required to be brought into Government Account without delay in accordance with the prescribed rules and regulations.

In view of the volume of expenditure particularly in regard to large projects and programmes, the system of

'Financial Advisers' has been established at the Union level. Prior to 1976 there were two separate functionaries, namely, Internal Financial Adviser and Associated Financial Adviser. A system of Integrated Financial Advisers is now operative. This system ensures the availability of in-house expert advice to administrative ministries and departments.

In fact, in regard to the financial powers which have been delegated to the ministries, the Financial Adviser acts as a part of the administrative ministry and his advice can be overruled by the ministry concerned. However, in those areas where the financial powers have not been delegated, this functionary acts on behalf of Ministry of Finance. In such areas he can be overruled only with the approval of the Ministry of Finance.

Internal Auditing

In India major importance is attached to the system of internal audit in Government. It is recognised that the continuing examination of the accounting and financial records, of systems and procedures, and of compliance with stated management policies, are essential elements of internal audit and a positive help to public administration. Accordingly each ministry and department of the Union Government has a special unit under the direct control and supervision of Financial Advisers.

All ministries and departments prepare their own internal audit manuals which detail the duties and functions of the internal audit unit. The findings of this unit are submitted to the permanent secretaries of the ministries concerned.

The audit by the CAG also lays a great deal of stress on the adequacy of internal audit systems. In those instances where the CAG is of the opinion that these systems need to be strengthened, appropriate comments and recommendations are made in his reports.

Audit Committee

In order to ensure speedy action on audit findings, instructions are issued by the Ministry of Finance either on its own initiative, or on the basis of suggestions by the CAG or on the recommendations of the Public Accounts Committee. These instructions require the (i) specification of time limits, (ii) designation of responsible officials and (iii) appointment of audit committees.

Reporting and Evaluation

Role of Executive Departments

Responsibility for monitoring the progress of expenditure against a Grant devolves on the executive which is ultimately responsible for keeping the expenditure within that Grant. In order to make control of expenditure against appropriations an operative reality, an efficient monitoring system has been established. A monthly return indicating separate plan and non-plan expenditure figures is prescribed to be furnished by the spending authorities. The consolidated information shows the sanctioned grant and the progressive total of expenditure incurred from month to month for a ministry as a whole. The system also provides for reconciliation of the departmental figures with the accounts figures. The ministries also obtain the details of physical progress of developmental schemes. These details include the budget provision, the progressive expenditure and the physical progress of each scheme in addition to the reasons for any financial and physical variations. The data relating to the progress of expenditure and the physical progress of the schemes are analysed every month and remedial action as considered necessary initiated.

The Accounts Officers under the Financial Adviser of each Ministry also keep a watch over the progress of expenditure and report to the departmental head concerned immediately if there is the likelihood of any grant being exceeded. Such financial surveillance provides an additional control mechanism to enable timely action by the executive.

Other Agencies

For effective control and monitoring of implementation of the developmental programmes and schemes, the Government of India has recently set up a separate Ministry of Programme Implementation. This ministry closely monitors the implemenation of major public sector projects and programmes. It also assists various other ministries in the preparation of Annual Action Plans and in the review of associated performance reports. For monitoring and generation of periodical reports, the system has been computerised by developing requisite data bases. The National Informatics Centre, set up as a nodal agency, has developed several data bases and continuously monitor all plan and non-plan programmes through a computer network known as NICNET which provides the data required by various users. The main users of such data presently are the Prime Minister's Office, Planning Commission and Ministry of Programme Implementation. The computer network is being extended to cover district treasuries in the States as well.

National Accounting System

One of the most distinctive features of the system of Government Accounts in India is the minute elaboration of the financial transactions of Government. Both receipts and payments, are differentiated and classified in detail. Further, the uniform classification of transactions enables financial comparisons between Union and State governments.

The following three developments are worth mentioning in this context:

1. In view of major public investments by way of plan outlay, government accounts were required to reflect clearly the expenditures incurred on various schemes, programmes and projects, i.e. to conform with plan heads of expenditure.
2. The Parliament and State Legislatures in addition to the general public, became increasingly conscious about government accountability.
3. The government, as a policy maker and as a manager of national finances, became more conscious about the use of government accounts as a tool for obtaining adequate and timely inputs for the purposes of evaluation, remedial action and future policy decisions.

These developments resulted in the government accounting authorities making the following responses:

(i) Preparation of aggregate accounts [Finance and Appropriation Accounts] with not only adequate financial and accounting data but *(a)* with a critical analysis of the financial performance of the government, *(b)* highlighting deviations from the expenditure incurred in contravention of approved appropriations, and *(c)* verifying the veracity of explanations offered by the executing agencies; and

(ii) Greater use of EDP methods for the purposes of accelerating the process of availability of final accounts and for quick retrieval of need-based information.

The major information inputs provided by the accounting authorities to the government are in the form of:- *(a)* Monthly and Annual Accounts, *(b)* Finance Accounts, *(c)* Appropriation Accounts and, additionally *(d)* Combined Finance and Revenue Accounts.

Type

The government accounts in India are kept on a cash basis. Therefore, only actual receipts and payments during the financial year are taken into account with no outstanding liabilities or accrued income included. All cash appropriations lapse at the close of the financial year.

Although the government accounts are maintained on cash basis, a need has been felt for maintaining the relevant accounts on a commercial basis (reflecting accrual accounting) in the case of those government departments where functions are purely or largely of a commercial nature. For this purpose proforma accounts are kept on commercial accounting principles for those commercial units under a ministry or department. For the major government commercial departments-such as Railways, and Posts and Telecommunications-detailed capital and revenue accounts are prepared and presented separately. This enables the public to see the complete picture inter alia about cost of services rendered and the return from investments.

While the question of government accounts being maintained on an accrual basis was being discussed and considered, it lost a great deal of its relevance in view of the emergence of a very large public sector in India. In compliance with the policy of the government to have a planned economy, massive investments have been made by the Government in various public enterprises. Since a large segment of governmental activity of a commercial, industrial and trading nature is being carried out by public enterprises based on commercial principles, the objective of accrual accounting is inherent in the model adopted.

Classification of Transactions

The conventional pattern of classification followed organisational lines, consisting mainly of the listing of receipts by various types of taxes, and expenditures by reference to the spending department rather than to its objects or purposes. With the phenomenal growth and diversity in the functions of governments involving huge outlays, accounts acquired a new dimension. Accordingly the necessity for a more meaningful classification of transactions for presentation of government operations in terms of functions, programmes and activities became increasingly apparent. A study team subsequently established by the Government of India, with the Deputy Comptroller and Auditor General as convenor investigated the feasibility of devising a uniform classification for the budget, accounts and plan, and of presenting the objectives and purposes of government expenditure clearly in terms of functions, programmes and activities.

Following the recommendations, the classification of transactions on a function-cum-programme basis was introduced from 1 April 1974. While the functional approach to classification is now well established, the divergence between plan programmes and accounting classification increased over the years. To bring about a closer correlation between plan schemes and Accounts Heads, the government constituted a committee which included a representative of CAG to review the existing classification and rationalise the Account Heads where required. As a result of this review in consultation with the CAG, the new accounting classification came into force from 1 April 1987.

While the basic principles and broad structure of accounts were retained, certain new sub-sectors were introduced, a new coding pattern was devised and other changes initiated so that expenditure on plan programmes could be extracted directly from the accounts. The list of Major and Minor Heads of Accounts of Union and States published by the Government of India gives the relevant details.

Main Divisions of Accounts

Following constitutional requirements government accounts are maintained in the following three categories:

Part I Consolidated Fund

Part II Contingency Fund

Part III Public Account

In Part I, there are two main divisions of the Consolidated Fund. The first division comprises the section 'Receipt heads (Revenue Account)' dealing with the proceeds of taxation and other receipts classed as revenue and the section 'Expenditure heads (Revenue Account)' dealing with expenditure met therefrom. The second division comprises the following sections :

a. The section 'Receipt heads (Capital Account)' which deals with receipts of a Capital nature which cannot be applied as a set off to Capital Expenditure;

b. The section 'Expenditure heads (Capital Account)' which deals with expenditure met usually from borrowed funds with the object either of increasing concrete assets of a material and permanent character or of reducing recurring liabilities. It also includes receipts of a Capital nature intended to be applied as set off to Capital expenditure; and

c. The sections 'Public Debt' and 'Loans and Advances',

which comprise loans raised and their re-payments such as internal debt, external debt and their recoveries.

In Part II, the transactions connected with the Contingency Fund set up by the Government of India or of a State are recorded. To complete the classification, Part III shows transactions relating to Debt (other than those included in Part I), 'Deposits', 'Advances', 'Remittances' and 'Suspense'.

Within each of the divisions and sections of the consolidated fund, the various transactions are grouped into sectors, such as 'General Services', 'Social Services' and 'Economic Services', These sectors have sub-sectors before their division into Major Heads of Account. In Part II- (Contingency Fund), there is a single Major Head to accommodate all transactions of the Contingency Fund. In the case of Part III (Public Account), transactions are grouped according to sectors and sub-sectors which are further sub-divided into Major Heads of Account.

Accounting Standards

As is already mentioned, the Constitution envisages that the accounts of the Union and the States are to be kept in such a form as the President may on the advice of the CAG prescribe. The word 'form' has a comprehensive meaning so as to include the prescription not only of the broad form in which the accounts are to be kept but also the appropriate heads under which certain transactions or classes of transactions have to be entered. Accordingly accounting standards have been established in rules and regulations mandated by the Union Government on the advice of the CAG. As regards the accounts of public enterprises and departmental commercial organisations, accounting standards are prescribed by the Indian Companies Act and professional accounting bodies. The Institute of Chartered Accountants of India accordingly has issued accounting standards which are implemented where relevant in this context. A representative of the CAG is generally associated with the standards setting process.

Production of the Accounts

Initially the CAG had the responsibility of compiling and maintaining the accounts of the Union and the States. He has now been relieved of this responsibility for the Union. The annual accounts in relation to Railways, Defence, Post and Telecommunications are produced by the respective departments of the Government of India. The Appropriation Accounts of the remaining departments and the Finances

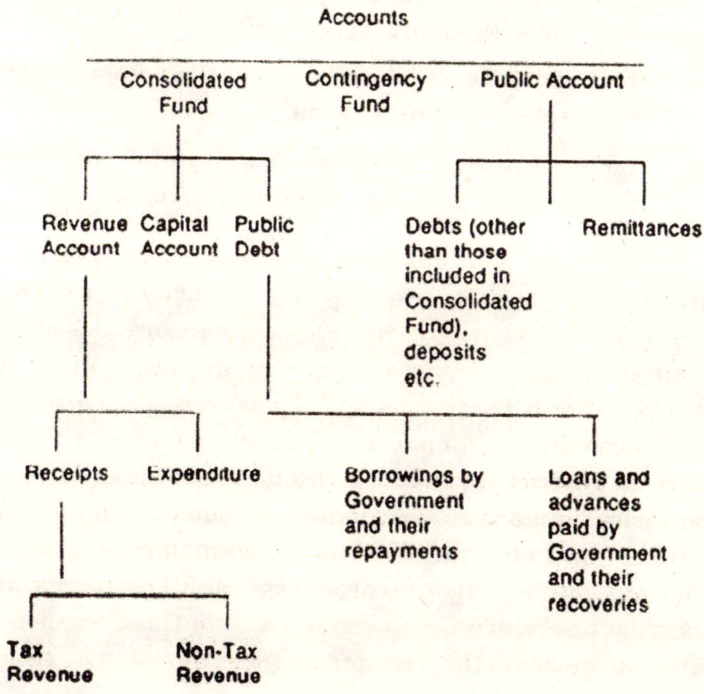

Accounts of the Government of India as a whole are produced by the Ministry of Finance. Responsibility for the production of the annual accounts of the State Governments is vested in the Accountants General, who are officers under the CAG.

Steps in the Accounting Progress

In view of the vast size of the country and widespread activities of the government, both at the Union and the State levels, the task of maintaining Government Accounts is indeed a formidable one. The process involves:

a. initial recording of accounting transactions, their classification with reference to a function or activity, their correlation with the administrative ministry/ department, i.e. the appropriate control centre, and their consolidation;

b. their matching with legally approved appropriations (to enable legislatural scrutiny); and

c. the analysis and presentation of this data to serve as a management tool to the two governments.

Accounts, as elsewhere, are a systematic record of various activities and functions expressed in financial terms and maintained by activity centres. Such accounts are classified as initial accounts. In the States they are maintained at the level of Sub-Treasuries and Treasuries. (A Treasury corresponds broadly to one administrative unit of a State known as 'District' and each 'District' has a number of Sub-Treasuries broadly corresponding to sub-divisions of a District). In India the Treasuries were formerly very important units of the fiscal system, and the points at which the public accounts originated. Into these financial centres were paid the receipts of government and from them were disbursed payments on behalf of the Government. Until the introduction of a new system (discussed later) and marked spread of government-owned banks, Treasuries and Sub-Treasuries were widely dispersed, functioning as bankers to the government, with the Reserve Bank of India at the apex. Later another major bank of the country (State Bank of India) commenced operations with many branches as a supplementary agency of the Reserve Bank of India. The cash balances of the Treasuries formed part of the Government Account.

It is remarkable that after 1975, two major developments took place :

1. The cash functions of the Treasuries and Sub-Treasuries were largely entrusted to government owned banks and their branches, and
2. With the establishment of a separate departmental accounting organisation in respect of the Union Government Civil Departments, the functions of the Treasuries and Sub- Treasuries at the Union level were largely taken over by the Pay and Accounts Offices. These offices are functionally under the control of the Permanent Secretaries of the Government, but administratively they are governed by the new department, viz. Indian Civil Accounts Department under the Ministry of Finance.

Remarkably, prior to 1976 responsibility for compiling and consolidating the accounts was not vested in executive departments but in the Accountants General under the aegis of the CAG (except in the case of Defence Department, Railways and a few other departments). With the formation of the new departmental accounting organisation, the responsibility of the Accountants General to maintain the accounts of Union Civil Departments was transferred to the former.

Before these developments took place, the revenue and other receipts and the payments made from Treasuries were recorded and compiled into two separate accounts for the transanctions of (i) the Union Government, and (ii) the State Governments. The classification of each item of receipt and payment according to its functional and administrative unit was made by the departmental offices. A list of payments (supported by payment vouchers) was sent by the Treasury Officers to the Accountant General twice a month and that of receipts once a month. Detailed rules were framed for the payment of moneys into and withdrawal of moneys from the Treasuries and their accounting. In the case of departments-such as Railways, Posts and Telegraphs, Defence, Public Works and Forest-the receipts realised were paid into the Treasuries in total and accounted for only as receipts of those departments. The detailed accounts of such receipts were kept by the departmental offices concerned. Similarly, sums withdrawn from the Treasuries (or a linked bank) by those departmental offices appeared in the Treasury accounts merely as payments on behalf of those departments-detailed accounts being maintained by the departmental offices.

From the initial accounts supported by payment vouchers rendered by the various treasuries and other departmental offices, the Accountants General compiled and consolidated the accounts in the form of Appropriation and Finance Accounts. The accounting position changed considerably after 1976. While the Accountants General, as functionaries of the CAG, are still compiling and maintaining the final Government Accounts at the State level, the responsibility at the Union level no longer lies with the Accountants

General. This has been transferred to a separate functionary, namely, the Controller General of Civil Accounts. Similarly functions of the Treasuries and Sub-treasuries, as recipients and disbursers of cash, have largely been transferred to the banks, while at the Union level the Treasuries have practically ceased to play any effective fiscal role.

The Government Accounts have necessarily to comply with the budgetary structure of the country. Since budgets in India are on an annual basis, governmental transactions are also finalised in the accounts on an annual basis. However, the government Accounts of each financial year are kept open for a certain period in the following year for adjusting transactions which took place in the previous financial year. This is considered necessary in order to allow certain inter-departmental adjustments, corrections of misclassifications, clearance of certain transitory heads (Suspense Heads), and other relevant adjustments.

Format of the Public Accounts

FINANCE ACCOUNTS : These accounts show the receipts and outgoings of the government for the year, together with the financial results disclosed by the revenue and capital accounts, the accounts relating to public debt, and liability and assets of the government. The Finance Accounts are generally prepared in two parts:

Part I - Summarised Statements

Part II - Detailed Accounts and Other Statements.

APPROPRIATION ACCOUNTS : These are accounts of the expenditure, voted and charged, of the government for each financial year compared with the amounts of the voted grants and appropriations charged for different purposes as specified in the schedules appended to the

Appropriation Acts. These accounts are complementary to the above accounts of the annual receipts and disbursements of government (Finance Accounts).

COMBINED FINANCE AND REVENUE ACCOUNTS OF THE CENTRAL AND STATE GOVERNMENTS IN INDIA : These present the accounts of all governments in India on a common and comparable basis. They are prepared by the CAG, mainly from the figures contained in the respective Finance Accounts of the governments concerned.

Monitoring Mechanisms

With the advent of the planned era in India following national independence, there was a major growth of economic development and social welfare activities. This growth necessitated an attendant increase in both revenue and capital expenditure, and in receipts and borrowings to match such expenditure. These new responsibilities of the government and the complex nature of its expanded activities called for a change in the nature and scope of audit. Consequently audit by the SAI has evolved from an accountancy and regularity check to evaluation of the end results of the operations of government, including considerations of economy, efficiency and effectiveness.

The audit by.the SAI is conducted under a Planned Programme covering the accounts, systems, procedures, projects and programmes on the basis of the documents and information submitted to the Indian Audit and Accounts Department. Field audits of the various organisations involved are an essential part of the overall programme. The initial audit findings are taken up with the appropriate authorities for remedial action through audit notes and inspection reports. Important audit findings, performance reviews of projects and programmes, and comprehensive appraisals of public enterprises and other bodies and authorities are processed for inclusion in the reports of the CAG which are laid before the Parliament or the State Legislatures as the case may be. Apart from the certification of the Appropriation Accounts and Finance Accounts of the Union and of 25 States and submission of separate audit reports on about 260 statutory corporations and other autonomous bodies for which the CAG is the sole auditor, the CAG brings out a large number of reports every year. These reports are of the following categories:

Union	*States*
Civil	Civil
Defence	Receipts
Railways	Commercial
Posts and Telecommunications	Autonomous Bodies
Direct Taxes	
Indirect Taxes	
Scientific Departments	
Autonomous Bodies	
Commercial	

The reports of the CAG after presentation to the legislature concerned are remitted to the related committees of Parliament and Slate Legislatures for consideration and appropriate recommendations to the executive for remedial action which is further followed up by the committees.

The Parliamentary Committees

Though Parliament itself does not govern the country, it exercises supervision over executive action in various ways through the purposive use of parliamentary procedures and a system of committees, although there is no constitutional provision for such committees of Parliament. As mentioned earlier, Parliament has set up three financial committees, viz. Public Accounts Committee (PAC), Committee on Public Undertakings (COPU) and the Estimates Committee, to assist effective parliamentary control over public finance.

The PAC examines the accounts showing the appropriation of sums granted by the House fort he expenditure of the Government of India, the annual finance accounts of the Government and such other accounts laid before the House as the Committee may think fit. Since 1962-63 the Committee has also examined the revenue receipts.

In scrutinising the Appropriation Accounts of the Government of India and the Report of the Comptroller and Auditor Genera! thereon, it is the duty of the Committee to satisfy itself that :

a. the moneys shown in the accounts as having been disbursed were legally available for, and applicable to, the service or purpose to which they have been applied or charged;
b. expenditure conforms to the authority which governs it; and
c. every reappropriation has been made in accordance with the provisions made in this regard under rules established by competent authority.

Even though the Parliament discusses the budget estimates for a sufficiently long period, there is often neither the time nor the flexibility to discuss the details and the technical aspects of the estimates. The Estimates Committee was therefore constituted to examine the estimates. The functions of this committee are detailed in Section 5.1 of this chapter.

Thirdly, COPU examines the reports and accounts of the public undertakings, including the audit reports of the CAG thereon. It is the function of this Committee to see whether the affairs of the public undertaking are being managed in accordance with sound business principles and prudent commercial practices.

The reports of the various committees are presented to the Parliament. The Government is required to inform the PAC/COPU within six months of the action taken by it on the recommendations of the committees. The committees, in turn, consider the Government's replies and present their further report known as the 'Action Taken Reports' incorporating their views on the action taken by the Government.

An adhoc committee, known as the Railway Convention Committee, is also constituted to review the rate of dividend which is payable by the railway undertaking to the general revenues in addition to other ancilliary matters in connection with railway finances vis-a-vis general finances, and make recommendations thereon.

Other Agencies

The Department of Public Enterprises of the Government of India analyses and monitors the annual performance of each public enterprise within the jurisdiction of COPU and submits to the government and parliament a combined annual performance appraisal of the public enterprises.

The Planning Commission undertakes selective monitoring covering major projects/programmes and important sectors. It also reviews the progress of the plan each year mainly in financial and some times in physical terms based on the detailed information obtained from central ministries and state governments during the formulation of the annual plan for the next year. The results of this review are given in the annual plan document. In addition the Commission brings out the mid term review of the Five Year Plans.

Conclusion

In India financial accountability and fiscal management systems covering budgeting, accounting and auditing, have evolved over more than a century.

This evolution has been in response to the changes in the political, social and economic environments nationally during this period. However the budget as an instrument of planned development and accounting as an aid to decision-making are relatively new concepts. Similarly, the transformation of audit from a relatively simple device to ensure mere regularity of government expenditure against budget appropriations in a colonial situation to an important organ of the democratic polity, engaged in sophisticated performance evaluation of public financial operations in a planned economy, is a phenomenon of post-Independent India.

Future reforms in the systems will have to address, among other things, the development of comprehensive management accounting and information systems capable of achieving effective financial control and accountability. With the vast increase in the financial transactions and their reflective activity centres adequate and reliable internal audit arrangements have to be instituted or strengthened. Further, a climate conducive to appropriate administrative responsiveness to the requirements of effective financial management, accounting and auditing will have to be created.

With the changing world economic scenario under the sway of LPG, budgetig in India may accommodate suitable modifications accordingly.

6

Budget in Parliament

In the preceding chapter, we have given an elaborate account of Budget preparation in India. In the present chapter we will give a brief account of passing the budget in Parliament.

With the emergence of Welfare State, Governments have come to look after virtually every sphere of human life. They have to perform manifold functions from maintaining law and order, protecting their territories to implementation of plans for economic and social betterment. Besides, they provide a variety of social services like education, health, employment and housing to the people. Needless to say, Government require adequate resources to discharge these functions effectively. Where is this money to come from and who is to sanction the funds? The necessary funds are mobilised from the country's resources by way of taxes both direct and indirect, loans both long-term and short-term, to meet the Governmental expenditure. In India, the principal sources of revenue are customs and excise duties and Income-tax on individuals and companies.

Why Budget?

It is not as if the Government can tax, borrow and spend money the way it likes. Since there is a limit to the resources, the need for proper budgeting arises to allocate scarce resources to various Governmental activities. Every item of expenditure has to be well thought out and total outlay worked out for a specific period. Prudent spending is essential for the stability of a Government and proper earnings are a pre-requisite to wise spending. Hence, planned expenditure and accurate foresight of earnings are *sine-qua-non* of sound Governmental finance.

Parliamentary Control Over Finance

Ours is a Parliamentary system of Government based on Westminster model. The Constitution has, therefore, vested the power over the purse in the hands of chosen representatives of the people thus sanctifying the principle 'no taxation without representation'. Preparation of Budget for the approval of the Legislature is a Constitutional obligation of the Government both at the Centre and the State levels. Legislative prerogative over taxation, legislative control over expenditure and executive initiative in financial matters are some of the fundamental principles of the system of Parliamentary financial control.

There are specific provisions in the Constitution of India incorporating these tenets. For example, article 265 provides that 'no tax shall be levied or collected except by authority of law'; no expenditure can be incurred except with the authorisation of the Legislature (article 266); and President shall, in respect of every financial year, cause to be laid before Parliament, Annual Financial Statement (article 112). These provisions of our Constitution make the Government accountable to Parliament.

The Budget

The 'Annual Financial Statement', laid before both the Houses of Parliament constitutes the Budget of the Union

Government. This statement takes into account a period of one financial year. The financial year commences in India on 1st April each year. The statement embodies the estimated receipts and expenditure of the Government of India for the financial year.

Demands for Grants

The estimates of expenditure included in the Budget and required to be voted by Lok Sabha are in the form of Demands for Grants. These Demands are arranged Ministry-wise and a separate Demand for each of the major services is presented. Each Demand contains first a statement of the total grant and then a statement of the detailed estimate divided into items.

Railway Budget

The Budget of the Indian Railways is presented separately to Parliament and dealt with separately, although the receipts and expenditure of the Railways form part of the Consolidated Fund of India and the figures relating to them are included in the 'Annual Financial Statement'.

Presentation

In India, the Budget is presented to Parliament on such date as is fixed by the President. The Budget speech of the Finance Minister is usually in two parts. *Part A* deals with general economic survey of the country while *Part B* relates to taxation proposals. General Budget was earlier being presented at 5 P.M. on the last working day of February, but since 1999 the General Budget is being presented at 11 A.M. on the last working day of February, i.e. about a month before the commencement of the Financial year except in the year when General Elections to Lok Sabha are held. In an election year, Budget may be presented twice—first to secure Vote on Account for a few months and later in full.

The General Budget is presented in Lok Sabha by the Minister of Finance. He makes a speech introducing the Budget and it is only in the concluding part of his speech that the proposals for fresh taxation or for variations in the existing taxes are disclosed by him. The 'Annual Financial Statement' is laid on the Table of Rajya Sabha at the conclusion of the speech of the Finance Minister in Lok Sabha.

Budget Documents

Alongwith the 'Annual Financial Statement' Government presents the following documents: an Explanatory Memorandum briefly explaining the nature of receipts and expenditure during the current year and the next year and the reasons for variations in the estimates for the two years, the Books of Demands showing the provisions Ministry-wise and a separate Demand for each Department and service of the Ministry. The Finance Bill which deals with the taxation measures proposed by Government is introduced immediately after the presentation of Budget. It is accompanied by a memorandum explaining the provisions of the Bill and their effect on the finances of the country.

Vote on Account

The discussion on the Budget begins a few days after its presentation. In a democratic set-up, Government is anxious to give Parliament full opportunity to discuss the budgetary provisions and the various proposals for taxation. Since Parliament is not able to vote the entire budget before the commencement of the new financial year, the necessity to keep enough finance at the disposal of

Government in order to allow it to run the administration of the country remains. A special provision is, therefore, made for "Vote on Account" by which Government obtains the Vote of Parliament for a sum sufficient to incur expenditure on various items for a part of the year.

Normally, the Vote on Account is taken for two months only. But during election year or when it is anticipated that the main Demands and Appropriation Bill will take longer time than two months, the Vote on Account may be for a period exceeding two months.

Discussion

The Budget is discussed in two stages in Lok Sabha. First, there is the General Discussion on the Budget as a whole. This lasts for about 4 to 5 days. Only the broad outlines of the Budget and the principles and policies underlying it are discussed at this stage.

Consideration of the Demands by Standing Committees of Parliament

After the first stage of General Discussion on both Railway as well as General Budget is over, the House is adjourned for a fixed period. During this period, the Demands for Grants of various Ministries/Departments including Railways are considered by concerned Standing Committees (Rule 331G). These Committees are required to make their reports to the House within specified period without asking for more time.

The system of consideration of Demands for Grants by the Standing Committees was introduced from the Budget for the year 1993-94. The Standing Committee consists of 45 Members, 30 from Lok Sabha and 15 from Rajya Sabha. The reports of the Standing Committees are of persuasive nature (Rule 331N). The report shall not suggest anything of the nature of cut motions.

After the reports of the Standing Committees are presented to the House, the House proceeds to the discussion and Voting on Demands for Grants, Ministry-wise. The time for discussion and Voting of Demands for Grants is allocated by the Speaker in consultation with the Leader of the House. On the last day of the allotted days, the Speaker puts all the outstanding Demands to the Vote of the House. This device is popularly known as 'guillotine'. Lok Sabha has the power to assent to or refuse to give assent to any Demand or even to reduce the amount of Grant sought by Government. In Rajya Sabha there is only a General Discussion on the Budget. It does not vote on the Demands for Grants. Only so much of the amount is subject to the vote of Lok Sabha as is not a "charged" expenditure on the Consolidated Fund of India.

The "charged" expenditure includes the emoluments of the President and the salaries and allowances of the Chairman and Deputy Chairman of Rajya Sabha and the Speaker and Deputy Speaker of Lok Sabha, Judges of Supreme Court, Comptroller and Auditor General of India and certain other items specified in the Constitution of India. Discussion in Lok Sabha on 'charged' expenditure is permissible but such expenditure is not voted by the House. Members have full opportunity to criticise the budgetary provisions during the course of discussion as also to make suggestions for improving the financial position of the country.

Cut Motions

Motions for reduction to various Demands for Grants are made in the form of Cut Motions seeking to reduce the sums sought by Government on grounds of economy or difference of opinion on matters of policy or just in order to voice a grievance.

Appropriation Bill

After the General Discussion on the Budget proposals and Voting on Demands for Grants have been completed, Government introduces the Appropriation Bill. The Appropriation Bill is intended to give authority to Government to incur expenditure from and out of the Consolidated Fund of India. The procedure for passing this Bill is the same as in the case of other money Bills.

Finance Bill

The Finance Bill seeking to give effect to the Government's taxation proposals which is introduced in Lok Sabha immediately after the presentation of the General Budget, is taken up for consideration and passing after the Appropriation Bill is passed. However, certain provisions in the Bill relating to levy and collection of fresh duties or variations in the existing duties come into effect immediately on the expiry of the day on which the Bill is introduced by virtue of a declaration under the Provisional Collection of Taxes Act. Parliament has to pass the Finance Bill within 75 days of its introduction.

Supplementary/Excess Grants

No expenditure in excess of the sums authorised by Parliament can be incurred without the sanction of Parliament. Whenever a need arises to incur extra expenditure, a Supplementary estimate is laid before Parliament. If any money has been spent on any service during a financial year in excess of the amounts granted for that service and for that year, the Minister of Finance/

Railways presents a Demand for Excess Grant. The procedure followed in Parliament in regard to Supplementary/Excess Grants is more or less the same as is adopted in the case of estimates included in the General Budget.

Budget of a State/Union Territory Under President's Rule

Budget of a State under President's rule is presented to Lok Sabha. The procedure followed in regard to the Budget of the Union Government is followed in the case of State Budget also with such variations or modifications, as the Speaker may make.

7

Union Budget of India 2010

Herein this chapter, first we will present the main highlights of the Union Budget 2010. A critical appraisal of the budget will be presented thereafter.

MAIN HIGHLIGHTS

- The Indian economy was facing grave uncertainty. Growth had started decelerating when the interim and full budget for 2009-10 were presented.
- At home there was added uncertainty because of subnormal southwest monsoon.
- Yet, the economy now in a far better position than it was eight years ago.
- India weathered the economic crisis well and emerged from the global slowdown faster than any other country.
- First challenge before the government is to quickly revert to high GDP growth path of 9%.
- Expects 10% economic growth in the near future.
- Second challenge is to harness economic growth to make it more inclusive and consolidate gains.
- Third challenge is to overcome weakness in

government's public delivery mechanism; a long way to go in this.

- Impressive recovery in the past few months. Can witness faster recovery in the coming months.
- Food security has been strengthened. But bottleneck of the public delivery mechanism can hold us back.
- Fiscal year 2009-10 was challenging for the economy.
- Focus shifted to non-governmental actors and an enabling government. Government now concentrates on supporting and delivering services to the poorer sections.
- Economy stabilised in the first quarter of 2009 itself.
- 18.5% manufacturing growth in December was the highest in two decades.
- Figures for merchandise exports for January encouraging after turnaround in November and December last year.
- Double digit food inflation last year due to bad monsoon and drought-like conditions.
- Government conscious of the price rise and taking steps to tackle it.
- Erratic monsoon and drought-like conditions forced supply-side bottleneck that fuelled inflation.
- Need to review stimulus imparted to economy last year to overcome the recession.
- Need to ensure that the demand-supply imbalance is managed.
- Need to make growth more broad-based.
- Need to review public spending and mobilise resources.

- Status paper on public debt within six months.
- Government hopes to implement direct tax code from April 2011.
- Earnest endeavour to implement general sales tax in April 2011.
- Government will raise Rs25,000 crore from divestment of its stake in state-owned firms.
- Kirit Parekh report on fuel price deregulation will be taken up by petroleum minister Murli Deora in due course.
- Nutrient-based fertiliser subsidy scheme to come into force from April 1 this year.
- Nutrient-based fertiliser subsidy will reduce volatility of subsidy and also reduce it.
- Market capitalisation of five public-sector undertakings listed since October increased by 3.5 times.
- FDI inflows steady during the year. Government has taken series of steps to simplify FDI regime. Intends to make FDI policy user friendly by compling all guidelines into one document.
- Government has decided to set up apex-level Financial
- Stability and Development Council.
- RBI considering issuing banking licences to private companies. Non-banking finance companies will also be considered if they meet the criteria.
- Government to provide Rs16,500 crore to public-sector banks to maintain tier-I capital.
- Government to continue interest subvention of 2% for one more year for exports covering handicrafts,

carpets, handlooms and small and medium enterprises.

- Government to provide Rs300 crore to organise 60,000 pulse and oilseed villages and provide integrated intervention of watershed and related programmes.
- Rs200 crore provided for climate-resilient agriculture initiative.
- Government committed to ensuring continued growth ofspecial economic zones
- Need to take firm view on opening up of the retail sector.
- Deficit in foodgrains storage capacity to be met with private-sector participation.
- Period for repayment of loans by farmers extended by six months to June 30, 2010, in view of the drought and floods in some parts of the country.
- Interest subvention for timely repayment of crop loans raised from 1% to 2%, bringing the effective rate of interest to 5%.
- Road transport allocation raised by 13% to Rs19,894 crore.
- Proposal to maintain thrust of upgrading infrastructure in rural and urban areas. IIFCL authorised to refinance infrastructure projects.
- Rs1,73,552 crore provided for infrastructure development.
- Allocation for railways fixed at Rs16,752 crore, an increase of Rs950 crore over the last financial year.
- Government proposes to set up Coal Development Regulatory Authority.

- Mega power plant policy modified to lower cost of generation; allocation to power sector more than doubled to Rs5,130 crore in 2010-11.
- Government favours competitive bidding for coal blocks for captive power plants.
- Rs500 crore allocated for solar and hydro projects for the Ladakh region in Jammu & Kashmir.
- Clean Energy Fund to be created for research in new energy sources.
- Allocation for new and renewable energy ministry increased by 61% to Rs1,000 crore.
- One-time grant of Rs200 crore provided to Tirupur textile cluster in Tamil Nadu.
- Allocation for National Ganga River Basin Authority doubled to Rs500 crore.
- Alternative port to be developed at Sagar Island in West Bengal.
- Draft of Food Security Bill ready, to be placed in the public domain soon.
- Outlay for social sectors pegged at Rs1,37,674 crore, accounting for 37% of the total plan allocation.
- Plan allocation for school education raised from Rs26,800 crore to Rs31,036 crore in 2010-11.
- 25% of plan outlay earmarked for rural infrastructure development.
- Plan allocation for health and family welfare increased to Rs22,300 crore from Rs19,534 crore.
- For rural development, Rs66,100 crore have been allocated.

- Allocation for National Rural Employment Guarantee Authority stepped up to Rs40,100 crore in 2010-11.
- Indira Awas Yojana's unit cost raised to Rs45,000 in the plains and Rs48,500 in hilly areas.
- Allocation for urban development increased by 75% to Rs5,400 crore in 2010-11.
- 1% interest subvention loan for houses costing up to Rs20 lakh extended to March 31, 2011; Rs700 crore provided.
- Allocation for development of micro and small-scale sector raised from Rs1,794 crore to Rs2,400 crore.
- Rs1,270 crore provided for slum development programme, marking an increase of 700%.
- Government to set up National Social Security Fund with initial allocation of Rs1,000 crore to provide social security to workers in the unorganised sector.
- Government to contribute Rs1,000 per annum to each account holder under the new pension scheme.
- Exclusive skill development programme to be launched for textile and garment-sector employees.
- Allocation for woman and child development increased by 80%
- Plan outlay for the social justice ministry raised by 80% to Rs4,500 crore.
- Plan allccation for minority affairs ministry raised from Rs1,740 crore to Rs2,600 crore.
- Financial-Sector Legislative Reforms Committee to be set up.
- Rs1,900 crore allocated for Unique Identification Authority of India.

- A unique identity symbol will be provided to the rupee in line with the US dollar, British pound sterling, euro and Japanese yen.
- Defence allocation pegged at Rs1,47,344 crore in 2010-11 against Rs1,41,703 crore in the previous year. Of this, capital expenditure would account for Rs60,000 crore.
- Planning Commission to prepare integrated action plan for
- Naxal-affected areas to encourage "misguided elements" to eschew violence and join the mainstream.
- Gross tax receipts pegged at Rs7,46,656 crore for 2010-11, non-tax revenues at Rs1,48,118 crore.
- Total expenditure pegged at Rs11.8 lakh crore, an increase of 8.6%.
- Fiscal deficit at 5.5%.
- Fiscal deficit seen at 4.8% and 4.1% in 2011-12 and 2012–13, respectively.
- Non-plan expenditure pegged at Rs37,392 crore and plan expenditure at Rs7,35,657 crore in budget estimates. Proposed increase of 15% in plan expenditure and 6% in non-plan expenditure.
- Cash subsidy for fuel and fertiliser instead of previous practice of bonds to continue.
- Fiscal deficit pegged at 6.9% in 2009-10 as against 7.8% in the previous fiscal.
- Government's net borrowing to be Rs3,45,010 crore for 2010-11.
- Income-tax department ready with two-page Saral-2 returns form for individual salaried assesses.

- Personal income-ax rates pruned:
  - Income up to Rs1.6 lakh — nil
  - Income above Rs1.6 lakh and up to Rs5 lakh — 10%
  - Income above Rs5 lakh and up to Rs8 lakh — 20%
  - Income above Rs8 lakh — **30%**
- Additional deduction of Rs20,000 allowed on long-term infrastructure bonds for income-tax payers; this is above Rs1 lakh on savings instruments allowed already.
- Investment-linked tax deductions to be allowed to two-star hotels anywhere in the country.
- Weighted deduction of 125% for payments to approved associations doing social and statistical research.
- One-time interim relief to housing and real-estate sector.
- Businesses with a turnover of up to Rs60 lakh and professionals earning up to Rs15 lakh to be exempted from the obligation to audit their accounts.
- Housing projects allowed to be completed in five years instead of four to avail of tax breaks.
- Revenue loss of Rs26,000 crore on direct tax proposals.
- Central excise duty on all non-petroleum products raised to 10% from 8%.
- FM increases customs duty on crude oil to 5%, on diesel and petrol to 7.5%, and on other petroleum products to 10%.
- Structural changes in excise duties on cigarettes, cigars, and cigarillos.

- Clean energy cess of Rs50 per ton to be levied on coal produced in India.
- Concessional excise duty of 4% on solar cycle-rickshaws.
- Balloons exempted from central excise duty.
- Customs and central excise proposals to result in a net revenue gain of Rs43,500 crore.
- More services to be brought under the service tax net.
- Certain accredited news agencies exempted from payment of service tax.
- Net revenue gain from tax proposals pegged at Rs20,500 crore.

SUMMARY OF UNION BUDGET 2010-11

The Union Budget this year has aimed to focus on inclusive growth and insuring food security. These concerns for aam aadami have gone hand in hand with credible measures for improving investment climate, strengthening infrastructure and fiscal consolidation. As the country looks to 'quickly revert to high GDP growth path' in the wake of 'uncertain times', concerns for inclusive growth targeting the disadvantaged sections form the defining features of the Budget.

Many new initiatives have been introduced for sustained and inclusive growth. These include setting up of Mahila Kisan Sashaktikaran Pariyojana, Financial Stability and Development Council, Gold Regulatory Authority, Technical Advisory Group for Unique Projects, National Mission for Delivery of Justice and Legal Reforms, Independent Evaluation Office and National Clean Energy Fund.

Presenting the Union Budget 2010-11 in the Lok Sabha today, the Finance Minister Shri Pranab Mukherjee, said that three challenges would continue to engage the Indian policy planners for next few years. The first challenge is to quickly revert to the high GDP growth path of 9% and then find the means to cross the double digit growth barrier. The second challenge is to consolidate recent gains in making development more inclusive. The third challenge is to remove weaknesses at different levels of governance and to improve public delivery mechanism. The Budget, therefore, focuses on fiscal consolidation, making growth more broad-based and ensuring that supply-demand imbalances are better managed.

The Minister expressed the hope that the economy will reach 10% growth in not too distant a future. The Minister explained that after a fall in GDP growth in 2008-09 to 6.7%, the growth has built up and 7.2% growth is expected in 2009-10. The Minister said that the recovery is very encouraging as it has come about despite negative growth in agriculture sector. The growth rate in manufacturing in December 2009 was 18.5%, the highest in past two decades. Similarly, there are also signs of a turnaround in the merchandise exports with a positive growth in November and December 2009 after a decline in about twelve successive months.

Expressing concern at the emergence of double digit food inflation, the Minister said that the Government has set in motion steps in consultation with the State Chief Ministers to bring down the inflation in the next few months and ensure better management of food security.

The Minister said that now that the recovery has taken roots, there is a need to review public spending, mobilize resources and gear them towards building the productivity of the economy.

The government will follow the recommendations of the Thirteenth Finance Commission by capping the government debt. The Commission has recommended a capping of the combined debt of the Centre and the States at 68% of the GDP to be achieved by 2014-15.

For the first time, the Government would target an explicit reduction in its domestic public debt-GDP ratio. A status paper would be brought out within six months, giving a detailed analysis of the situation and a road map for curtailing the overall public debt. This would be followed by an annual report on the subject.

The Finance Minister expressed the hope that a broad consensus would be achieved on the Direct Tax Code and the Goods and Service Tax (GST) and these would be introduced from April 2011.

Investment Environment's Improvement

The Finance Minister said that a number of steps have been taken to simplify the Foreign Direct Investment (FDI) regime. The government also intends to make the FDI policy user-friendly by consolidating all prior regulations and guidelines into one comprehensive document. This would enhance clarity and predictability of our FDI policy to foreign investors, he said.

With a view to strengthen and institutionalize the mechanism for maintaining financial stability, Government has decided to set up an apex-level Financial Stability and Development Council. It would monitor macro prudential supervision of the economy, including the functioning of large financial conglomerates.

Towards strengthening the banking system, the Budget provides Rs.16500 crore as Tier-I capital. It would ensure that the Public Sector Banks are able to attain a minimum 8% Tier-I Capital by March 2011. Further capital would also be infused into the Regional Rural Banks (RRBs). The Minister also informed that the RBI is considering giving some additional banking licenses to private sector players. Non Banking Financial Companies could also be considered, if they meet the RBI's eligibility criteria.

Agriculture Growth

A four-pronged strategy would be followed to spur growth in agriculture sector. The elements of the strategy are (a) agricultural production; (b) reduction in wastage of produce; (c) credit support to farmers; and (d) a thrust to the food processing sector.

The Budget provides Rs.400 crore for extending the green revolution to the eastern region of the country comprising Bihar, Chattisgarh, Jharkhand, Eastern UP, West Bengal and Orissa, with the active involvement of Gram Sabhas and the farming families.

60,000 'pulses and oil seed villages' will be organized in rainfed areas with an outlay of Rs.300 crore during 2010-11. This will provide water harvesting, watershed management and soil health facilities to enhance to productivity of dryland farming areas. Another Rs.200 crore have been provided in the Budget for conservation farming.

To improve the storage capacity of food grains, Food Corporation of India is being allowed to hire godowns from private parties for a guaranteed period of seven years. This period so far was five years.

The target for farm credit is being raised to Rs.3,75,000 crore in 2010-11 from Rs.3,25,000 crore in the current year.

The period for repayment of loans under the Debt Waiver and Debt Relief Scheme is being extended by six months to June 30,2010.

The interest subvention for timely repayment of crop loans is being raised from 1% to 2%. Thus, the effective rate of interest for crop loans for farmers who repay their crop loan as per schedule will now be 5% per year.

Five more Mega Food Parks will be set up in addition to the 10 already being established. External Commercial Borrowings will henceforth be available for cold storage, farm level pre-cooling and preservation and storage of agricultural and allied produce marine products and meat.

Infrastructure

The Budget provides Rs.1,73,552 crore for infrastructure, accounting for over 46% of the total Plan allocation.The allocation for road transport is being increased by over 13% from Rs 17,520 crore to Rs.19,894 crore.

Disbursement for infrastructure by India Infrastructure Finance Company Ltd(IIFCL) is expected to reach Rs.20,000 crore in 2010-11 as against Rs.9,000 crore this year. Refinancing of bank landing to infrastructure projects by IIFCL is expected to be more than double in 2010-11.

Energy

The Plan allocation for power sector is being more than doubled from Rs.2,230 crore in 2009-10 to Rs.5,130 crore in 2010-11.

A Coal Regulatory Authority is proposed to be set up for creating level playing field in the coal sector and resolving various issues.

The Plan outlay for New and Renewal Energy Ministry is being increased by 61% from Rs. 620 crore to Rs.1,000 crore, especially to support the ambitious solar energy programme.

Inclusive Development

Stating that inclusive development is an act of faith for the UPA government, the Finance Minister said that after the Right to Information, Right to Work and Right to Education, the government is now ready with the draft Food Security Bill. A sums of Rs.1,37,674 crore, representing 37% of the total outlay, will be spent on social sector programmes.

Plan Allocation for school education is being increased from Rs.26,800 crore to Rs.31,036 crore to support the children's rights to free and compulsory education. In addition, States will have an access to Rs. 3,675 crore for elementary education under the Finance Commission grant for 2010-11.

It has been decided to provide appropriate banking facilities to habitations having population in excess of 2000 by March 2012. It is also proposed to extend insurance and other services to the targeted beneficiaries. These provisions are expected to cover 60,000 habitations.

Rs.66,100 crore have been provided for Rural Development. Mahatma Gandhi National Rural Employment Guarantee Scheme gets Rs.40,100 crore and Bharat Nirman Programme, Rs.48,000 crore.

Indira Awas Yojana gets Rs.10,000 crore. The unit cost under this scheme is being raised to Rs.45,000 in plain areas and Rs.48500 in hilly areas to cover the increase in cost of construction of houses.

The allocation to Backward Region Grant Fund is being enhanced by 26% from Rs.5,800 crore to Rs.7,300 crore. An additional Central assistance of Rs.1,200 crore is being provided for drought mitigation in the Bundelkhand region.

Swarna Jayanti Shahari Rozgar Yojana gets 75% increase in allocation from Rs.3,060 crore to Rs.5,400 crore. In addition, the allocation for Housing and Urban Poverty Alleviation is also being raised from Rs.850 crore to Rs.1,000 crore in 2010-11.

The 1% interest subvention on housing loans upto Rs.10 lakh (where the cost of the house does not exceed Rs.20 lakh) provided in the Budget for 2009-10 has been extended by another year.

Rajiv Awas Yojana, a scheme for housing to slum dwellers and urban poor, gets a huge jump in allocation from Rs.150 crore last year to Rs.1,270 crore in 2010-11.

It has been decided to set up a National Social Security Fund for unorganized sector workers with an initial allocation of Rs.1,000 crore. This fund will support schemes for weavers, toddy tappers, rickshaw pullers, bidi workers etc.

The Rashtriya Swasthya Bima Joyana is being extended to all Mahatma Gandhi NREGA beneficiaries who have worked for more than 15 days during the preceding financial year.

The Swavalamban initiative started last year, under which the government contributes Rs.1,000 per year to each New Pension Scheme (NPS) account, will now be available for another three years.

Plan outlay for Women and Child Development is being stepped up by 50%. A Mahila Kisan Sashaktikaran Pariyojana is being launched to meet the specific needs of women farmers.

The Plan outlay of Ministry of Social Justice and Empowerment gets a boost of 80% to Rs.4,500 crore. Besides supporting the programmes for the target beneficiaries, the Ministry will be able to raise the rates for scholarship schemes for SC and OBC students. Similarly, the Ministry of Minority Affairs allocation has been raised by 50% to Rs.2,600 crore.

Strengthening Transparency and Public Accountability

The government proposes to set up a Financial Sector Legislative Reforms Commission to rewrite and clean up the financial sector laws to bring them in line with the requirements of the sector.

Rs.1,900 crore has been allocated for the Unique Identification Authority of India.

A Technology Advisory Group for Unique Projects (TAGUP) is proposed to be set up under the Chairmanship of Shri Nandan Nilekani for creation of reliable and secure IT projects.

Defence gets an allocation of Rs.1,47,344 crore. As a one time confidence building measure in Jammu and Kashmir about 2000 youths will be recruited as constable in five Central Para-Military forces in 2010. Adequate funds will be made available to support the action plan to be prepared by the Planning Commission for development of 33 left wing extremist affected districts.

An Independent Evaluation Office is to be set up to undertake impartial and objective assessment of various public programmes and improve the effectiveness of public interventions in Planning Commission.

A National Mission for Delivery of Justice and Legal Reforms is also to be set up.

Tax Proposals

The Finance Minister emphasized the need for continued Tax Reforms. The Tax Returns form are being simplified and the Income Tax Department is now ready to notify Saral-2 forms for individual salary tax payers. The Sevottam project started in four cities to provide a single window system for registration and grievance redressal will be extended to four more cities. Two more centres will be opened for bulk processing of Tax Returns. The Indirect Tax Administrations are being revamped to achieve the roll out of Goods and Services Tax (GST). Rs.1133 crore have been budgeted for a mission mode project to achieve this.

Major relief has been provided to individual tax payers by enhancing exemption limit and reducing tax in different slabs of personal income.. Deduction of an additional amount of Rs.20000 for investment in long term infrastructure bonds will be available in addition to the existing limit of Rs.1 lakh available for specified savings.

The surcharge on domestic companies is being reduced from 10% to 7.5%. However, the minimum alternate tax (MAT) is being increased from 15% to 18%.

Exemptions and deductions have been provided to increase spending on research.

The investment linked deduction to new hotels of two star category and above is being extended to give boost to investment in Tourism sector.

A one time interim relief is being provided to the housing and real estate sector by allowing pending projects to be completed within a period of five years instead of four years for claiming a deduction on their profits.

The Finance Minister has proposed to partially roll back the rate deduction in Central Excise duties and enhance the standard rate on all non-petroleum products from 8% to 10% ad valorem. The specific rates of duty applicable to Portland cement and cement clinker are also being adjusted upwards proportionately. Similarly, the ad valorem component of excise duty on large cars, multi-utility vehicles and sports utility vehicles which was reduced as part of the first stimulus package, is being increased by 2 percentage points to 22%.

The basic duty of 5% on crude petroleum; 7.5% on diesel and petrol and 10% on other refined products is being enhanced. The Central Excise Duty on petrol and diesel is being enhanced by Rs.1 per litre.

Excise duty on non-smoking tobacco is being enhanced. In addition a compounded levy scheme is being introduced by chewing tobacco and branded unmanufactured tobacco based on the capacity of pouch making machines.

A number of duty concessions are being proposed to support agriculture and allied sector. Mechanised handling systems in warehouses will get project import status with a concessional import duty of 5%. Installation and commissioning of such equipment will be fully exempt from service tax. Concessional duty will also be applicable for cold storages, food processing units, specified equipment for food preservation etc. The concessional import duty to specified machinery for use in the plantation sector is being further extended upto March 2011. Testing and certification of agricultural seed is being exempt from service tax.

Tax exemptions have been announced for equipment used in solar systems and wind energy system, LED lights, electric cars, cycle rickshaw, mobile phone components and certain medical equipment.

The rate of tax on services has been retained at 10%.

Budget Estimates

The Budget Estimates 2010-11 provides for a total expenditure of Rs. 11,08,749 crore. Out of this, Rs 3,73,092 crore is plan expenditure and Rs.7,35,657 crore is non-plan expenditure. The plan expenditure has increased by 15% while there is only 6% in increase in non-plan expenditure.

The total receipt are estimate Rs.7,46,651 crore.

The Fiscal deficit is pegged at 5.5%. In the Medium Term Fiscal Policy Statement being presented along with other Budget documents in the House today, the rolling targets for fiscal deficit are pegged at 4.8% and 4.1% for 2011-12 and 2012-13, respectively. These projections improve upon the recommendations of the Thirteenth Finance Commission.

REFERENCES

"Key features of Union Budget 2009-2010". Indian Express. Jul 06, 2009. http://www.expressindia.com/latest-news/Key-features-of-Union-Budget-20092010/485658/.

"Union Budget 2010: Renewable energy sector earmarked Rs 380 crore more". Economic Times. 26 Feb 2010. http://economictimes.indiatimes.com/news/economy/policy/Union-Budget-2010-Renewable-energy-sector-earmarked-Rs-380-crore-more/articleshow/5621897.cms.

8

Government Debt and Allied Issues

"Debt is the slavery of the free."

—*Publilius Syrus*

In fact, Government debt is money (or credit) owed by any level of government; either central government, federal government, municipal government or local government. By contrast, annual government deficit refers to the difference between government receipts and spending in a single year. Debt of a sovereign government is called sovereign debt.

As the government draws its income from much of the population, government debt is an indirect debt of the taxpayers. Government debt can be categorized as internal debt, owed to lenders within the country, and external debt, owed to foreign lenders. Governments usually borrow by issuing securities, government bonds and bills. Less creditworthy countries sometimes borrow directly from supranational institutions.

Basically a broader definition of government debt considers all government liabilities, including future pension payments and payments for goods and services the government has contracted but not yet paid. Another common division of government debt is by duration until repayment is due. Short term debt is generally considered to be one year or less, long term is more than ten years. Medium term debt falls between these two boundaries.

Government and Sovereign Bonds

A government bond is a bond issued by a national government, and often denominated in the country's domestic currency. Bonds issued by national governments in foreign currencies are normally referred to as sovereign bonds. Government bonds are theoretically risk-free bonds, because governments can, up to a point, raise taxes, reduce spending, or simply print more money to redeem the bond at maturity. Investors in sovereign bonds denominated in foreign currency have the additional risk that the issuer may be unable to obtain foreign currency to redeem the bonds.

Municipal, Provincial, or State Bonds

Municipal bonds, "munis" in the United States, are debt securities issued by local governments (municipalities).

Denominated in Reserve Currencies

Governments borrow money in a currency in which the demand for debt securities is strongest. An advantage of issuing bonds in a currency such as the US dollar, the pound sterling, or the euro is that many investors wish to invest in such bonds. Countries such as the United States, France and Germany have only issued in their domestic currency. Relatively few investors are willing to invest in currencies that do not have a long track record of stability.

A disadvantage for a government issuing bonds in a foreign currency is that there is a risk that it will not be able to obtain the foreign currency to pay the interest or redeem the bonds. In 1997/1998, during the Asian financial crisis, this became a serious problem when many countries were unable to keep their exchange rate fixed due to speculative attacks.

Risk

Lending to a national government in the country's own sovereign currency is often considered "risk free" and is done at a so-called "risk-free interest rate". This is because, up to a point, the debt and interest can be repaid by raising tax receipts (either by economic growth or raising tax rates), a reduction in spending, or failing that by simply printing more money. Some economists argue that, in an economy near the full employment, this would increase inflation and reduce the value of the invested capital. An extreme example of this is provided by Weimar Germany of the 1920s which suffered from hyperinflation due to its government's inability to pay the national debt deriving from the costs of World War I. In practice, the market interest rate tends to be different for debts of different countries. An example is in borrowing by different European Union countries denominated in euros. Even though the currency is the same in each case, the yield required by the market is higher for some countries' debt than for others.

This reflects the views of the market on the relative solvency of the various countries and the likelihood that the debt will be repaid.

Notably, a politically unstable state is anything but risk-free as it may, being sovereign, cease its payments. Examples of this phenomenon include Spain in the 16th and 17th centuries, which nullified its government debt seven times during a century, and revolutionary Russia of 1917 which refused to accept the responsibility for Imperial Russia's foreign debt. Another political risk is caused by external threats. It is most uncommon for invaders to accept responsibility for the national debt of the annexed state or that of an organization it considered as rebels. For example, all borrowings by the Confederate States of America were left unpaid after the American Civil War.

On the other hand, in the modern era, the transition from dictatorship and illegitimate governments to democracy does not automatically free the country of the debt contracted by the former government. Today's highly developed global credit markets would be less likely to lend to a country that negated its previous debt, or might require punishing levels of interest rates that would be unacceptable to the borrower. U.S. Treasury bonds denominated in U.S. dollars are often considered "risk free" in the U.S. This disregards the risk to foreign purchasers of depreciation in the dollar relative to the lender's currency. In addition, a risk-free status implicitly assumes the stability of the US government and its ability to continue repayments during any financial crisis.

Lending to a national government in a currency other than its own does not give the same confidence in the ability to repay, but this may be offset by reducing the exchange rate risk to foreign lenders. On the other hand, national debt in foreign currency cannot be disposed of by starting a hyperinflation; and this increases the credibility of the debtor.

Usually small states with volatile economies have most of their national debt in foreign currency. For countries in the Eurozone, the euro is the local currency, although no single state can trigger inflation by creating more currency. Lending to a local or municipal government can be just as risky as a loan to a private company, unless the local or municipal government has sufficient power to tax. In this case, the local government could to a certain extent pay its debts by increasing the taxes, or reduce spending, just as a national one could.

Further, local government loans are sometimes guaranteed by the national government, and this reduces the risk. In some jurisdictions, interest earned on local or municipal bonds is tax-exempt income, which can be an important consideration for the wealthy.

Clearing and Defaults

Public debt clearing standards are set by the Bank for International Settlements, but defaults are governed by extremely complex laws which vary from jurisdiction to jurisdiction. Globally, the International Monetary Fund can take certain steps to intervene to prevent anticipated defaults.

It is sometimes criticized for the measures it advises nations to take, which often involve cutting back on government spending as part of an economic austerity regime. In triple bottom line analysis, this can be seen as degrading capital on which the nation's economy ultimately depends. Those considerations do not apply to private debts, by contrast: credit risk (or the consumer credit rating) determines the interest rate, more or less, and entities go bankrupt if they fail to repay. Governments cannot really go bankrupt (and suddenly stop providing services to citizens), thus a far more complex way of managing defaults is required. Smaller jurisdictions, such as cities, are usually guaranteed by their regional or national levels of government. When New York City during the 1960s declined into what would have been a bankrupt status (had it been a private entity) by the early 1970s, a "bailout" was required from New York State and the United States.

In general such measures amount to merging the smaller entity's debt into that of the larger entity and thereby giving it access to the lower interest rates the large one enjoys. The larger entity may then assume some agreed-upon oversight in order to prevent recurrence of the problem.

Structure

In the dominant economic policy generally ascribed to theories of John Maynard Keynes, sometimes called Keynesian economics, there is tolerance for fairly high levels of public debt to pay for public investment in lean times, which, if boom times follow, can then be paid back from rising tax revenues.

As this theory gained global popularity in the 1930s, many nations took on public debt to finance large infrastructural capital projects — such as highways or large hydroelectric dams. It was thought that this could start a virtuous cycle and a rising business confidence since there would be more workers with money to spend. Some have argued that the greatly increased military spending of World War II really ended the Great Depression. Of course, military expenditures are based upon the same tax (or debt) and spend fundamentals as the rest of the national budget, so this argument does little to undermine Keynesian theory.

Indeed, some have suggested that significantly higher national spending necessitated by war essentially confirms the basic Keynesian analysis (see Military Keynesianism). (There is much debate as to what exactly ended the Great Depression, in particular from Austrian Economics.) Nonetheless, the Keynesian scheme remained dominant, thanks in part to Keynes' own pamphlet *How to Pay for the War*, published in the United Kingdom in 1940. Since the war was being paid for, and being won, Keynes and Harry Dexter White, Assistant Secretary of the United States Department of the Treasury, were, according to John Kenneth Galbraith, the dominating influences on the Bretton Woods agreements.

These agreements set the policies for the BIS, IMF, and World Bank, the so-called *Bretton Woods Institutions*, launched in the late 1940s for the last two (the BIS was founded in 1930).

These are the dominant economic entities setting policies regarding public debt. Due to their role in setting policies for trade disputes, the General Agreement on Tariffs and Trade (GATT) and World Trade Organization also have immense power to affect foreign exchange relations, as many nations are dependent on specific commodity markets for the balance of payments they require to repay debt.

As such, understanding the structure of public debt and analyzing its risk requires one to:

- Assess the expected value of any public asset being constructed, at least in future tax terms if not in direct revenues. A choice must be made about its status as a public good — some public "assets" end up as public bads, such as nuclear power plants which are extremely expensive to decommission — these costs must also be worked in to asset values.
- Determine whether any public debt is being used to finance consumption, which includes all social assistance and all military spending.
- Determine whether triple bottom line issues are likely to lead to failure or defaults of governments — say due to being overthrown.

- Determine whether any of the debt being undertaken may be held to be odious debt, which might permit it to be disavowed without any effect on a country's credit status. This includes any loans to purchase "assets" such as leaders' palaces, or the people's suppression or extermination. International law does not permit people to be held responsible for such debts — as they did not benefit in any way from the spending and had no control over it.
- Determine if any future entitlements are being created by expenditures — financing a public swimming pool for instance may create some right to recreation where it did not previously exist, by precedent and expectations.

Scale

Global debt is of great concern since interest payments can often place great demands on governments and individuals.

This has led to calls for universal debt relief for poorer countries. A less extreme measure is to permit civil society groups in every nation to buy the debt in exchange for minority equity positions in community organizations.

Even in dictatorships, the combination of banks and civil society power could force land reform and overthrow unaccountable governments, since the people and banks would be aligned against the oppressive government. Using a debt to GDP ratio is one of the most accepted measures of assessing a nation's debt. For example, in theory one of the criteria of admission to the European Union's Euro currency is that a country's debt should not exceed 60% of that country's GDP.

Problems

Sovereign debt problems have been a major public policy issue since World War II, including the treatment of debt related to that war, the developing country "debt crisis" in the 1980s, and the shocks of the 1998 Russian financial crisis and Argentina's default in 2001.

So called developing countries, for example Yugoslavia and least developed countries often had less government debt (perhaps because they were unable to borrow on world markets) until their break up and the coming of democracy, when the new governments started to borrow money from the IMF. Croatia has a government debt of $47 billion today while the whole of Yugoslavia (six times as many people as Croatia) in 1980 had debt of $14 billion.

Implicit Debt

Government "implicit" debt is the promise by a government of future payments from the state. Usually this refers to long term promises of social payments such as pensions and health expenditure; not promises of other expenditure such as education or defense (which are largely paid on a "quid pro quo" basis to government employees and contractors).

A problem with these implicit government insurance liabilities is that it is hard to cost them accurately, since the amounts of future payments depend on so many factors. First of all, the social security claims are not "open" bonds or debt papers with a stated time frame, "time to maturity", "nominal value", or "net present value". In the United States, as in most other countries, there is no money earmarked in the government's coffers for future social insurance payments. This insurance system is called PAYGO (pay-as-you-go) as opposed to save and invest. Furthermore, population projections predict that when the "baby boomers" start to retire the working population in the United States, and in many other countries, will be a smaller percentage of the population than it is now, for many years to come. This will increase the burden on the country of these promised pension and other payments - larger than the 65% of GDP that it is now. The "burden" of the government is what it spends, since it can only pay its bills through taxes, debt, and increasing the money supply (government spending = tax revenues + change in government debt held by public + change in monetary base held by the public). "Government social benefits" paid by the United States government during 2003 totalled $1.3 trillion.

GOVERNMENT SPENDING

Government spending or government expenditure is classified by economists into three main types. Government acquisition of goods and services for current use to directly satisfy individual or collective needs of the members of the community is classed as government final consumption expenditure. Government acquisition of goods and services intended to create future benefits, such as infrastructure investment or research spending, is classed as government investment (gross fixed capital formation), which usually is the largest part of the government gross capital formation. Acquisition of goods and services is made through own production by the government (using the government's labour force, fixed assets and purchased goods and services for intermediate consumption) or through purchases of goods and services from market producers.

Government expenditures that are not acquisition of goods and services, and instead just represent transfers of money, such as social security payments, are called transfer payments. Government spending can be financed by seigniorage, taxes, or government borrowing. The first two types of government spending, namely government final consumption expenditure and government gross capital formation, together constitute one of the major components of gross domestic product.

John Maynard Keynes was one of the first economists to advocate government deficit spending as part of the fiscal policy response to an economic contraction. In Keynesian economics, increased government spending is thought to raise aggregate demand and increase consumption. Classical economists and Austrian economists, however, believe that increased government spending exacerbates an economic contraction by shifting resources from the private sector, which they consider productive, to the public sector, which they consider unproductive. According to Austrian economists, the reason the Great Depression lasted as long as it did was because of significant government spending and government regulation of the economy.

Government spending in the United States of America occurs at several levels of government, including primarily federal, state, and local governments. The United States Census Bureau publishes an overview of government spending every year in the Statistical Abstract of the United States.

In the most recent year for which actual spending for all levels of government has been reported, overall government spending for all levels of government in the United States of America was as follows:

United States Federal, State,and Local Government Spending Fiscal Year 2006

Function	*Amount(billion)*	*Percent GDP*
Overall government spending		
Federal, State, Local	$4,704.1	36.1
Spending by major government function		
Pensions	$747.1	5.7
Health Care	$783.8	6.0
Education	$900.8	6.9
Defense	$622.2	4.8
Welfare	$411.4	3.2
Interest	$312.3	2.4

Government spending expressed as a percent of Gross Domestic Product is based on a total of $13,015.5 billion for calendar year 2006 reported by the Bureau of Economic Analysis.

Federal Spending

As of September 2004 the U.S. Congressional Budget Office reported that federal government spending for 2004 was projected to be $2.293 trillion, or slightly less than 20% of the GDP. Of that, $159 billion was for net interest, $486 billion for defense, $492 billion for Social Security, $473 billion for Medicare and Medicaid, $191 billion for various welfare programs, $136 billion for "retirement and disability" benefits, and $64 billion was projected to be spent elsewhere.

There are two types of government spending — discretionary and mandatory. Discretionary spending, which accounts for roughly one-third of all Federal spending, includes money for things like the Army, FBI, the Coast

Guard, and highway projects. Congress explicitly determines how much to spend (or not spend) on these programs on an annual basis. Mandatory spending accounts for two-thirds of all government spending.

This kind of spending is authorized by permanent laws. It includes "entitlements" like Social Security, Medicare, and Food Stamps — programs through which individuals receive benefits based on their age, income, or other criteria. Spending levels in these areas are dictated by the number of people who sign up for these benefits, rather than by Congress.

State and Local Spending

The United States Census Bureau conducts a census of State and Local Government Finances every five years and updates the census every year. The latest fiscal year reported by the Census Bureau is 2006.

The United States Census Bureau publishes historical data series on government spending in the United States in its Statistical Abstract of the United States and in its special release of historical statistics in 1976 at the time of the US Bicentennial.

Over the last century starting overall government spending in the United States has increased substantially from about seven percent of GDP in 1902 to about 35 percent of GDP in 2010. Major spikes in spending occurred in World War I and World War II.

When broken down by major function, the history of government spending as a percent of GDP shows a slow and consistent increase in education spending; it shows the spikes in defense spending during World War I and World

War II, and the sustained high level maintained during the Cold War.

Spending on welfare shows a clear takeoff during the Great Depression and a modest decline following reform in 1996. Spending on pensions (primarily Social Security) begins to show up in the 1950s. Health care spending takes off after the birth of Medicare and Medicaid in the 1960s and shows sustained growth ever since.

Spending Patterns

In an interview with Charlie Rose, Milton Friedman noted that government spending declines fastest in the United States when Democrats control the executive branch while Republicans control the legislature.

GOVERNMENT OPERATIONS

This article aims to describe the financial expenditure associated with the operations and processes of world governments of all levels.

The scale to which government should exist and operate in the world is a matter of debate. Government spending in developed countries varies considerably but generally makes up between about 30% and 70% of their GDP. One major exception is the United States, where central government spending takes up less than 20% of GDP, although the combined spending of all administrations reach 36%.

Services

Government agencies may produce services like:

- Communications
- Education (e.g. community college)

- Emergency services
- Entertainment (e.g. Canadian Broadcasting Corporation)
- Entitlements
- Financial services
- Financing
- Fire fighting
- Healthcare
- Insurance
- Law
- Law enforcement
- Police
- Postal service
- Transport (e.g. government transportation)

Goods

Government agencies may produce goods like:

- Coal
- Electrical infrastructure
- Oil (e.g. Pemex)
- Roads, bridges, tunnels
- Sewers
- Steel
- Water infrastructure

Local Government

At the level of local government, territorial or other

authorities may set up government corporations such as "Local Authority Trading Enterprises" (LATEs).

Commonwealth of Nations

In monarchical commonwealth countries country-wide government corporations often use the style "crown corporation". Notable exceptions include both the state-owned enterprises and the crown entities in New Zealand. Examples of crown corporations include the Canadian Broadcasting Corporation (CBC) in Canada and Air Canada before it underwent privatisation. Cabinet ministers (ministers of the crown) often control the shares in such public corporations.

United States

In the United States, businesses that are government owned include Amtrak and the United States Postal Service. Many states have government owned businesses for operations as well. Generally speaking, a statute passed by a legislature specifically sets up a government owned company in order to undertake a specific public purpose with public funds or public property.

Privatization

Privatization is the transfer of ownership from the public sector (government) to the private sector (business).

INCOME DISTRIBUTION

Modern economists have also addressed this issue, but have been more concerned with the distribution of income across individuals and households. Important theoretical and policy concerns include the relationship between income inequality and economic growth.

In economics, income distribution is how a nation's total economy is distributed amongst its population.Income distribution has always been a central concern of economic theory and economic policy. Classical economists such as Adam Smith, Thomas Malthus and David Ricardo were mainly concerned with factor income distribution, that is, the distribution of income between the main factors of production, land, labour and capital.

The distribution of income within a community may be represented by the Lorenz curve. The Lorenz curve is closely associated with measures of income inequality, such as the Gini coefficient.

In the United States, income is distributed somewhat unequally, with those in the top two quintiles earning more than the bottom 60% combined. Yet, the distribution of income is not nearly as polarized as in many developing countries with most of America's earned income resting in the hands of the middle class.

Aggregate U.S. Household Income Distribution, 2007

Percentage of total US household income earned by income group

	10%	*20%*	*30%*	*40%*	*50%*
3.1%			less than $20,000 —	19.04% of all households	
8.1%			$20,000 to $37,500 —	19.45% of all households	
13.8%			$37,500 to $60,000 —	19.44% of all households	
22.3% —	$60,000 to $95,000			20.00% of all households	
40.8% —	$95,000 to $250,000 —	20.15% of all households			
11.9%			$250,000 or more -	1.92% of all households	

GOVERNMENT REVENUE

Government revenue is revenue received by a government. Its opposite is government spending. Government revenue is an important part of fiscal policy.

Revenue may be from various taxes or non-tax revenue (such as revenue from government-owned corporations or sovereign wealth funds).

REFERENCES

Hedlund, Stefan (2004). "Foreign Debt". *Encyclopedia of Russian History (reprinted in Encyclopedia.com).*

James Macdonald, *A Free Nation Deep in Debt: The Financial Roots of Democracy* (Princeton: Princeton University Press, 2006). 564 pp.

Niall Ferguson. *The Cash Nexus: Money and Power in the Modern World, 1700-2000* (New York: Basic, 2002).

Robert E. Wright, *One Nation Under Debt: Hamilton, Jefferson, and the History of What We Owe* (New York: McGraw Hill, 2008).

Robert Barro and Vittorio Grilli (1994), *European Macroeconomics*, Ch. 15-16. Macmillan.

9

Taxation in Budgeting

To tax is to impose a financial charge or other levy upon a taxpayer (an individual or legal entity) by a state or the functional equivalent of a state such that failure to pay is punishable by law. Taxes are also imposed by many subnational entities. Taxes consist of direct tax or indirect tax, and may be paid in money or as its labour equivalent (often but not always unpaid labour).

A tax may be defined as a "pecuniary burden laid upon individuals or property owners to support the government [...] a payment exacted by legislative authority." A tax "is not a voluntary payment or donation, but an enforced contribution, exacted pursuant to legislative authority" and is "any contribution imposed by government [...] whether under the name of toll, tribute, tallage, gabel, impost, duty, custom, excise, subsidy, aid, supply, or other name."

The legal definition and the economic definition of taxes differ in that economists do not consider many transfers to governments to be taxes. For example, some transfers to the public sector are comparable to prices. Examples include tuition at public universities and fees for utilities provided by local governments. Governments also obtain resources by creating money (e.g., printing bills and minting coins), through voluntary gifts (e.g., contributions to public universities and museums),by imposing penalties (e.g., traffic fines), by borrowing, and by confiscating wealth. From the view of economists, a tax is a non-penal, yet compulsory transfer of resources from the private to the public sector levied on a basis of predetermined criteria and without reference to specific benefit received.

Remarkably, in modern taxation systems, taxes are levied in money, but in-kind and *corvée* taxation are characteristic of traditional or pre-capitalist states and their functional equivalents. The method of taxation and the government expenditure of taxes raised is often highly debated in politics and economics.

Tax collection is performed by a government agency such as Canada Revenue Agency, the Internal Revenue Service (IRS) in the United States, or Her Majesty's Revenue and Customs (HMRC) in the UK. When taxes are not fully paid, civil penalties (such as fines or forfeiture) or criminal penalties (such as incarceration) may be imposed on the non-paying entity or individual.

Purposes and Effects

Funds provided by taxation have been used by states and their functional equivalents throughout history to carry out many functions. Some of these include expenditures on war, the enforcement of law and public order, protection of property, economic infrastructure (roads, legal tender, enforcement of contracts, etc.), public works, social engineering, and the operation of government itself. Governments also use taxes to fund welfare and public services.

These services can include education systems, health care systems, pensions for the elderly, unemployment benefits, and public transportation. Energy, water and waste management systems are also common public utilities. Colonial and modernizing states have also used cash taxes to draw or force reluctant subsistence producers into cash economies. Governments use different kinds of taxes and vary the tax rates. This is done to distribute the tax burden among individuals or classes of the population involved in taxable activities, such as business, or to redistribute resources between individuals or classes in the population. Historically, the nobility were supported by taxes on the poor; modern social security systems are intended to support the poor, the disabled, or the retired by taxes on those who are still working.

In addition, taxes are applied to fund foreign aid and military ventures, to influence the macroeconomic performance of the economy (the government's strategy for doing this is called its fiscal policy - see also tax exemption), or to modify patterns of consumption or employment within an economy, by making some classes of transaction more or less attractive. A nation's tax system is often a reflection of its communal values or/and the values of those in power. To create a system of taxation, a nation must make choices regarding the distribution of the tax burden—who will pay taxes and how much they will pay—and how the taxes collected will be spent. In democratic nations where the public elects those in charge of establishing the tax system, these choices reflect the type of community that the public and/or government wishes to create.

In countries where the public does not have a significant amount of influence over the system of taxation, that system may be more of a reflection on the values of those in power. The resource collected from the public through taxation is always greater than the amount which can be used by the government. The difference is called *compliance cost*, and includes for example the labour cost and other expenses incurred in complying with tax laws and rules.

The collection of a tax in order to spend it on a specified purpose, for example collecting a tax on alcohol to pay directly for alcoholism rehabilitation centres, is called hypothecation. This practice is often disliked by finance ministers, since it reduces their freedom of action. Some economic theorists consider the concept to be intellectually dishonest since (in reality) money is fungible.

Furthermore, it often happens that taxes or excises initially levied to fund some specific government programs are then later diverted to the government general fund. In some cases, such taxes are collected in fundamentally inefficient ways, for example highway tolls.

Some economists, especially neo-classical economists, argue that all taxation creates market distortion and results in economic inefficiency. They have therefore sought to identify the kind of tax system that would minimize this distortion. Also, one of every government's most fundamental duties is to administer possession and use of land in the geographic area over which it is sovereign, and it is considered economically efficient for government to recover for public purposes the additional value it creates by providing this unique service. Since governments also resolve commercial disputes, especially in countries with common law, similar arguments are sometimes used to justify a sales tax or value added tax.

Others (e.g. libertarians) argue that most or all forms of taxes are immoral due to their involuntary (and therefore eventually coercive/violent) nature. The most extreme anti-tax view is anarcho-capitalism, in which the provision of *all* social services should be voluntarily bought by the person(s) using them.

The Four "R"s

Taxation has four main purposes or effects: *Revenue, Redistribution, Repricing,* and *Representation.*

The main purpose is revenue: taxes raise money to spend on armies, roads, schools and hospitals, and on more indirect government functions like market regulation or legal systems. This is the most widely known function.

A second is redistribution. Normally, this means transferring wealth from the richer sections of society to poorer sections.

A third purpose of taxation is repricing. Taxes are levied to address externalities: tobacco is taxed, for example, to discourage smoking, and many peopleadvocate policies such as implementing a carbon tax.

A fourth, consequential effect of taxation in its historical setting has been representation. The American revolutionary slogan "no taxation without representation" implied this: rulers tax citizens, and citizens demand accountability from their rulers as the other part of this bargain. Several studies have shown that direct taxation (such as income taxes) generates the greatest degree of accountability and better governance, while indirect taxation tends to have smaller effects.

Proportional, Progressive, and Regressive

An important feature of tax systems is the percentage of the tax burden as it relates to income or consumption. The terms progressive, regressive, and proportional are used to describe the way the rate progresses from low to high, from high to low, or proportionally. The terms describe a distribution effect, which can be applied to any type of tax system (income or consumption) that meets the definition. A progressive tax is a tax imposed so that the effective tax rate increases as the amount to which the rate is applied increases. The opposite of a progressive tax is a regressive tax, where the effective tax rate decreases as the amount to which the rate is applied increases. In between is a proportional tax, where the effective tax rate is fixed, while the amount to which the rate is applied increases. The terms can also be used to apply meaning to the taxation of select consumption, such as a tax on luxury goods and the exemption of basic necessities may be described as having progressive effects as it increases a tax burden on high end consumption and decreases a tax burden on low end consumption.

Direct and Indirect

Taxes are sometimes referred to as direct taxes or indirect taxes. The meaning of these terms can vary in different contexts, which can sometimes lead to confusion. An economic definition, by Atkinson, states that "...direct taxes may be adjusted to the individual characteristics of the taxpayer, whereas indirect taxes are levied on transactions irrespective of the circumstances of buyer or seller." (A. B. Atkinson, *Optimal Taxation and the Direct Versus Indirect Tax Controversy,* 10 Can. J. Econ. 590, 592 (1977)). According to this definition, for example, income tax is "direct", and sales tax is "indirect". In law, the terms may have different meanings. In U.S. constitutional law, for instance, direct taxes refer to poll taxes and property taxes, which are based on simple existence or ownership. Indirect taxes are imposed on events, rights, privileges, and activities. Thus, a tax on the sale of property would be considered an indirect tax, whereas the tax on simply owning the property itself would be a direct tax. The distinction between direct and indirect taxation can be subtle, but can be important under the law.

Tax Burden

Law establishes from whom a tax is collected. In many countries, taxes are imposed on business (such as corporate taxes or portions of payroll taxes). However, who ultimately pays the tax (the tax "burden") is determined by the marketplace as taxes become embedded into production costs. Depending on how quantities supplied and demanded vary with price (the "elasticities" of supply and demand), a tax can be absorbed by the seller (in the form of lower pre-tax prices), or by the buyer (in the form of higher post-tax prices). If the elasticity of supply is low, more of the tax will be paid by the supplier. If the elasticity of demand is low, more will be paid by the customer.

And contrariwise for the cases where those elasticities are high. If the seller is a competitive firm, the tax burden flows back to the factors of production depending on the elasticities thereof; this includes workers (in the form of lower wages), capital investors (in the form of loss to shareholders), landowners (in the form of lower rents) and entrepreneurs (in the form of lower wages of superintendence). To illustrate this relationship, suppose the market price of a product is US$1.00, and that a $0.50 tax is imposed on the product that, by law, is to be collected from the seller. If the product is a luxury (in the economic sense of the term), a greater portion of the tax will be absorbed by the seller. This is because a luxury good has elastic demand which would cause a large decline in quantity demanded for a small increase in price.

Therefore in order to stabilise sales, the seller absorbs more of the additional tax burden. For example, the seller might drop the price of the product to $0.70 so that, after adding in the tax, the buyer pays a total of $1.20, or $0.20 more than he did before the $0.50 tax was imposed. In this example, the buyer has paid $0.20 of the $0.50 tax (in the form of a post-tax price) and the seller has paid the remaining $0.30 (in the form of a lower pre-tax price).

Taxation Levels

The first known system of taxation was in Ancient Egypt around 3000 BC - 2800 BC in the first dynasty of the Old Kingdom. Records from the time document that the Pharaoh would conduct a biennial tour of the kingdom, collecting tax revenues from the people. Other records are granary receipts on limestone flakes and papyrus. Early taxation is also described in the Bible. In Genesis (chapter 47, verse 24 - the New International Version), it states "But when the crop comes in, give a fifth of it to Pharaoh. The other four-fifths you may keep as seed for the fields and as food for yourselves and your households and your children." Joseph was telling the people of Egypt how to divide their crop, providing a portion to the Pharaoh. A share (20%) of the crop was the tax.

Later, in the Persian Empire, a regulated and sustainable tax system was introduced by Darius I the Great in 500 BC; the Persian system of taxation was tailored to each Satrapy (the area ruled by a Satrap or provincial governor). At differing times there were between 20 and 30 Satrapies in the Empire and each was assessed according to its supposed productivity.

It was the responsibility of the Satrap to collect the due amount and to send it to the emperor, after deducting his expenses (The expenses and the power of deciding precisely how and from whom to raise the money in the province, offer maximum opportunity for rich pickings.) The quantities demanded from the various provinces gave a vivid picture of their economic potential. For instance, Babylon was assessed for the highest amount and for a startling mixture of commodities - 1000 silver talents, four months supply of food for the army. India clearly, was already fabled for its gold; the province was to supply gold dust equal in value to the very large amount of 4680 silver talents. Egypt was known for the wealth of its crops; it was to be the granary of the Persian Empire (as later of Rome's) and was required to provide 120,000 measures of grain in addition to 700 talents of silver. This was exclusively a tax levied on subject peoples. Persians and Medes paid no tax, but, they were liable at any time to serve in the army.

In India, Islamic rulers imposed jizya starting in the 11th century. It was abolished by Akbar.

Quite a few records of government tax collection in Europe since at least the 17th century are still available today. But taxation levels are hard to compare to the size and flow of the economy since production numbers are not as readily available. Government expenditures and revenue in France during the 17th century went from about 24.30 million *livres* in 1600-10 to about 126.86 million *livres* in 1650-59 to about 117.99 million *livres* in 1700-10 when government debt had reached 1.6 billion *livres*. In 1780-89 it reached 421.50 million *livres*.

Taxation as a percentage of production of final goods may have reached 15% - 20% during the 17th century in places like France, the Netherlands, and Scandinavia. During the war-filled years of the eighteenth and early nineteenth century, tax rates in Europe increased dramatically as war became more expensive and governments became more centralized and adept at gathering taxes.

This increase was greatest in England, Peter Mathias and Patrick O'Brien found that the tax burden increased by 85% over this period. Another study confirmed this number, finding that per capita tax revenues had grown almost sixfold over the eighteenth century, but that steady economic growth had made the real burden on each individual only double over this period before the industrial revolution. Average tax rates were higher in Britain than France the years before the French Revolution, twice in per capita income comparison, but they were mostly placed on international trade. In France, taxes were lower but the burden was mainly on landowners, individuals, and internal trade and thus created far more resentment.

Taxation as a percentage of GDP in 2003 was 56.1% in Denmark, 54.5% in France, 49.0% in the Euro area, 42.6% in the United Kingdom, 35.7% in the United States, 35.2% in The Republic of Ireland, and among all OECD members an average of 40.7%.

Types of Taxation

In monetary economies prior to fiat banking, a critical form of taxation was seigniorage, the tax on the creation of money.

Other obsolete forms of taxation include:

- Scutage - paid in lieu of military service; strictly speaking a commutation of a non-tax obligation rather than a tax as such, but functioning as a tax in practice

- Tallage - a tax on feudal dependents
- Tithe - a tax-like payment (one tenth of one's earnings or agricultural produce), paid to the Church (and thus too specific to be a tax in strict technical terms). This should not be confused with the modern practice of the same name which is normally voluntary.
- Aids - During feudal times a feudal aid was a type of tax or due paid by a vassal to his lord.
- Danegeld - medieval land tax originally raised to pay off raiding Danes and later used to fund military expenditures.
- Carucage - tax which replaced the danegeld in England.
- Tax Farming - the principle of assigning the responsibility for tax revenue collection to private citizens or groups.

Some principalities taxed windows, doors, or cabinets to reduce consumption of imported glass and hardware. Armoires, hutches, and wardrobes were employed to evade taxes on doors and cabinets. In some circumstances, taxes are also used to enforce public policy like congestion charge (to cut road traffic and encourage public transport) in London. In Tsarist Russia, taxes were clamped on beards. Today, one of the most complicated taxation-systems worldwide is in Germany. Three quarters of the world's taxation-literature refers to the German system. There are 118 laws, 185 forms, and 96,000 regulations, spending €3.7 billion to collect the income tax. Today, governments of advanced economies of EU, North America, and others rely more on direct taxes, while those of developing economies of India, Africa, and others rely more on indirect taxes.

Tax Rates

Taxes are most often levied as a percentage, called the *tax rate*. An important distinction when talking about tax rates is to distinguish between the marginal rate and the effective (average) rate. The effective rate is the total tax paid divided by the total amount the tax is paid on, while the marginal rate is the rate paid on the next dollar of income earned. For example, if income is taxed on a formula of 5% from $0 up to $50,000, 10% from $50,000 to $100,000, and 15% over $100,000, a taxpayer with income of $175,000 would pay a total of $18,750 in taxes.

Tax calculation

(0.05*50,000) + (0.10*50,000) + (0.15*75,000) = 18,750

The "effective rate" would be 10.7%:

18,750/175,000 = 0.107

The "marginal rate" would be 15%.

Economics of Taxation

In economic terms, taxation transfers wealth from households or businesses to the government of a nation. The side-effects of taxation and theories about how best to tax are an important subject in microeconomics. Taxation is almost never a simple transfer of wealth. Economic theories of taxation approach the question of how to minimize the loss of economic welfare through taxation and also discuss how a nation can perform redistribution of wealth in the most efficient manner.

Deadweight Costs of Taxation

For goods supplied in a perfectly competitive market, tax reduces economic efficiency, by introducing a deadweight loss. In a perfect market, the price of a particular economic good adjusts to make sure that all trades which benefit both the buyer and the seller of a good occur. After introducing a tax, the price received by the seller is less than the cost to the buyer.

This means that fewer trades occur and that the individuals or businesses involved gain less from participating in the market. This destroys value, and is known as the 'deadweight cost of taxation'. The deadweight cost is dependent on the elasticity of supply and demand for a good.

Most taxes—including income tax and sales tax—can have significant deadweight costs. The only way to completely avoid deadweight costs in an economy which is generally competitive is to find taxes which do not change economic incentives, such as the land value tax, where the tax is on a good in completely inelastic supply, a lump sum tax such as a poll tax which is paid by all adults regardless of their choices, or a windfall profits tax which is entirely unanticipated and so cannot affect decisions.

Double Dividend Taxes

In some cases where the economy is not perfectly competitive, the existence of a tax can *increase* economic efficiency. If there is a negative externality associated with a good, meaning that it has negative effects not felt by the consumer, then the free market will trade too much of that good. By putting a tax on the good, the government can increase overall welfare as well as raising revenue in taxation. This is known as a 'double dividend'.

There are a wide range of goods where there is, or is claimed to be, a negative externality. Polluting fuels (like petrol), goods which incur public healthcare costs (such as alcohol or tobacco), and charges for existing 'free' public goods (like congestion charging) all offer the possibility of a double dividend. This type of tax is a Pigovian tax, sometimes colloquially known as a 'sin tax'. It is worthwhile noting that taxation is not necessarily the only, or the best, method of dealing with negative externalities.

Another concern is that the complicated tax codes of developed economies offer perverse economic incentives. The more details of tax policy there are, the more opportunities for legal tax avoidance and illegal tax evasion; these not only result in lost revenue, but involve additional deadweight costs: for instance, payments made for tax advice are essentially deadweight costs because they add no wealth to the economy.

Perverse incentives also occur because of non-taxable 'hidden' transactions; for instance, a sale from one company to another might be liable for sales tax, but if the same goods were shipped from one branch of a corporation to another, no tax would be payable. To address these issues, economists often suggest simple and transparent tax structures which avoid providing loopholes. Sales tax, for instance, can be replaced with a value added tax which disregards intermediate transactions.

Tax Incidence

Economic theory suggests that the economic effect of tax does not necessarily fall at the point where it is legally levied. For instance, a tax on employment paid by employers will impact on the employee, at least in the long run. The greatest share of the tax burden tends to fall on the most inelastic factor involved - the part of the transaction which is affected least by a change in price. So, for instance, a tax on wages in a town will (at least in the long run) affect property-owners in that area.

Costs of Compliance

Although governments must spend money on tax collection activities, some of the costs, particularly for keeping records and filling out forms, are borne by businesses and by private individuals. These are collectively called costs of compliance. More complex tax systems tend to have higher costs of compliance. This fact can be used as the basis for practical or moral arguments in favor of tax simplification (see, for example, FairTax), or tax elimination (in addition to moral arguments described above).

Kinds of Taxes

The Organisation for Economic Co-operation and Development (OECD) publishes perhaps the most comprehensive analysis of worldwide tax systems. In order to do this it has created a comprehensive categorisation of all taxes in all regimes which it covers:

Ad Valorem

An *ad valorem* tax is one where the tax base is the value of a good, service, or property. Sales taxes, tariffs, property taxes, inheritance taxes, and value added taxes are different types of ad valorem tax. An ad valorem tax is typically imposed at the time of a transaction (sales tax or value added tax (VAT)) but it may be imposed on an annual basis (property tax) or in connection with another significant event (inheritance tax or tariffs).

An alternative to ad valorem taxation is an excise tax, where the tax base is the quantity of something, regardless of its price. For example, in the United Kingdom, a tax is collected on the sale of alcoholic drinks that is calculated by volume and beverage type, rather than the price of the drink.

Bank Tax

A bank tax ("bank levy") is a proposed tax on banks. One of the earliest modern uses of the term "bank tax" occurred in the context of the Financial crisis of 2007–2010.

Capital Gains Tax

A capital gains tax is the tax levied on the profit released upon the sale of a capital asset. In many cases, the amount of a capital gain is treated as income and subject to the marginal rate of income tax. However, in an inflationary environment, capital gains may be to some extent illusory: if prices in general have doubled in five years, then selling an asset for twice the price it was purchased for five years earlier represents no gain at all. Partly to compensate for such changes in the value of money over time, some jurisdictions, such as the United States, give a favorable capital gains tax rate based on the length of holding. European jurisdictions have a similar rate reduction to nil on certain property transactions that qualify for the participation exemption. In Canada, 50% of the gain is taxable income. In India, Short Term Capital Gains Tax (arising before 1 year) is 10% flat rate of the gains and Long Term Capital Gains Tax is nil for stocks & mutual fund units held 1 year or more and 20% for any other assets held 3 years or more. If such a tax is levied on inherited property, it can act as a *de facto* probate or inheritance tax.

Consumption Tax

A consumption tax is a tax on non-investment spending, and can be implemented by means of a sales tax or by modifying an income tax to allow for unlimited deductions for investment or savings.

Corporation Tax

Corporate tax refers to a direct tax levied by various jurisdictions on the profits made by companies or associations and often includes capital gains of a company. Earnings are generally considered gross revenue less expenses. Corporate expenses that relate to capital expenditures are usually deducted in full (for example, trucks are fully deductible in the Canadian tax system, while a corporate sports car is only partly deductible). They are often deducted over the useful life of the asset purchase. Notably, accounting rules about deductible expenses and tax rules about deductible expense will differ at times, giving rise to book-tax differences. If the book-tax difference is carried over more than a year, it is referred to as a temporary difference, which then creates deferred tax assets and liabilities for the corporation, which are carried on the balance sheet.

Currency Transaction Tax

A currency transaction tax is a tax placed on a specific type of currency transaction for a specific purpose. This term has been most commonly associated with the financial sector, as opposed to consumption taxes paid by consumers. There are several types of currency transaction taxes that have been proposed, the most prominent being the Tobin tax and the Spahn tax. Most remain unimplemented concepts.

Environment Affecting Tax

This includes natural resources consumption tax, GreenHouse gas tax (Carbon tax), "sulfuric tax", and others. The stated purpose is to reduce the environmental impact by repricing.

Excises

Unlike an *ad valorem*, an excise is not a function of the value of the product being taxed. Excise taxes are based on the quantity, not the value, of product purchased. For example, in the United States, the Federal government imposes an excise tax of 18.4 cents per U.S. gallon (4.86¢/L) of gasoline, while state governments levy an additional 8 to 28 cents per U.S. gallon. Excises on particular commodities are frequently hypothecated. For example, a fuel excise (use tax) is often used to pay for public transportation, especially roads and bridges and for the protection of the environment.

A special form of hypothecation arises where an excise is used to compensate a party to a transaction for alleged uncontrollable abuse; for example, a blank media tax is a tax on recordable media such as CD-Rs, whose proceeds are typically allocated to copyright holders. Critics charge that such taxes blindly tax those who make legitimate and illegitimate usages of the products; for instance, a person or corporation using CD-R's for data archival should not have to subsidize the producers of popular music. Excises (or exemptions from them) are also used to modify consumption patterns (social engineering). For example, a high excise is used to discourage alcohol consumption, relative to other goods.

This may be combined with hypothecation if the proceeds are then used to pay for the costs of treating illness caused by alcohol abuse. Similar taxes may exist on tobacco, pornography, etc., and they may be collectively referred to as "sin taxes".

A carbon tax is a tax on the consumption of carbon-based non-renewable fuels, such as petrol, diesel-fuel, jet fuels, and natural gas. The object is to reduce the release of carbon into the atmosphere. In the United Kingdom, vehicle excise duty is an annual tax on vehicle ownership.

Expatriation Tax

An Expatriation Tax is a tax on some who renounce their citizenship of some governments. The most significant Expatriation Tax is one found in the USA.

The American Jobs Creation act of 2004, passed by the Republican-controlled government, amended section 877 of the Internal Revenue Code of the USA. Under the new law, any individual who has a net worth of $2 million or an average income-tax liability of $127,000 who renounces his or her citizenship and leaves the country is automatically assumed to have done so for tax avoidance reasons and is victim to severe tax laws.

Financial Activities Tax

As a regulatory response and proposal to the financial crisis of 2007-2010, on April 16, 2010, the IMF proposed three types of global taxes on banks: First, the "Financial Stability Contribution" is a straight tax on a bank's gross profits—before deducting compensation. It would initially be at a flat rate, this would eventually be refined so that riskier businesses paid more. Second, the "Financial Activities Tax" aims directly at excess bank profit and pay. The third, which was not endorsed by the IMF, but not ruled out as administratively difficult, is a financial transaction tax.

Financial Transaction Tax

A financial transaction tax is a tax placed on a specific type (or types) of financial transaction for a specific purpose (or purposes). This term has been most commonly associated with the financial sector, as opposed to consumption taxes paid by consumers.

There are several types of financial transaction taxes. Each has its own purpose. Some have already been implemented, and some remain unimplemented concepts. Concepts are found in various organizations and regions around the world. Some are domestic and meant to be used within one nation; whereas some are multinational.

Income Tax

An income tax is a tax levied on the financial income of persons, corporations, or other legal entities. Various income tax systems exist, with varying degrees of tax incidence. Income taxation can be progressive, proportional, or regressive. When the tax is levied on the income of companies, it is often called a corporate tax, corporate income tax, or corporation tax.

Individual income taxes often tax the total income of the individual (with some deductions permitted), while corporate income taxes often tax net income (the difference between gross receipts, expenses, and additional write-offs). The "tax net" refers to the types of payment that are taxed, which included personal earnings (wages), capital gains, and business income. The rates for different types of income may vary and some may not be taxed at all. Capital gains may be taxed when realized (e.g. when shares are sold) or when incurred (e.g. when shares appreciate in value).

Business income may only be taxed if it is significant or based on the manner in which it is paid. Some types of income, such as interest on bank savings, may be considered as personal earnings (similar to wages) or as a realized property gain (similar to selling shares). In some tax systems, personal earnings may be strictly defined where labor, skill, or investment is required (e.g. wages); in others, they may be defined broadly to include windfalls (e.g. gambling wins).

Personal income tax is often collected on a pay-as-you-earn basis, with small corrections made soon after the end of the tax year. These corrections take one of two forms: payments to the government, for taxpayers who have not paid enough during the tax year; and tax refunds from the government for those who have overpaid. Income tax systems will often have deductions available that lessen the total tax liability by reducing total taxable income. They may allow losses from one type of income to be counted against another. For example, a loss on the stock market may be deducted against taxes paid on wages. Other tax systems may isolate the loss, such that business losses can only be deducted against business tax by carrying forward the loss to later tax years.

Inheritance Tax

Inheritance tax, estate tax, and death tax or duty are the names given to various taxes which arise on the death of an individual. In United States tax law, there is a distinction between an estate tax and an inheritance tax: the former taxes the personal representatives of the deceased, while the latter taxes the beneficiaries of the estate. However, this distinction does not apply in other jurisdictions; for example, if using this terminology UK inheritance tax would be an estate tax.

Inflation Tax

An inflation tax is the economic disadvantage suffered by holders of cash and cash equivalents in one denomination of currency due to the effects of Expansionary monetary policy, which acts as a hidden tax that subtracts value from those assets. Many economists hold that the inflation tax affects the lower and middle classes more than the rich, as they hold a larger fraction of their income in cash, they are much less likely to receive the newly created monies before the market has adjusted with inflated prices, and more often have fixed incomes, wages or pensions.

Some argue that inflation is a regressive consumption tax. There are systemic effects of an expansionary monetary policy, which are also definitively taxing, imposing a financial charge on some as a result of the policy. Because the effects of monetary expansion or counterfeiting are never uniform over an entire economy, the policy influences capital transfers in the market, creating economic bubbles where the new monies are first introduced.

Economic bubbles increase market instability, and therefore increase investment risk, creating the conditions common to a recession. This particular tax can be understood to be levied on future generations that would have benefited from economic growth, and it has a 100% transfer cost (so long as people are not acting against their interests, increased uncertainty benefits no-one). One example of a strong supporter of this tax was the former Federal Reserve chair Beardsley Ruml.

Poll Tax

A poll tax, also called a *per capita tax*, or *capitation tax*, is a tax that levies a set amount per individual. It is an example of the concept of fixed tax. One of the earliest taxes mentioned in the Bible of a half-shekel per annum from each adult Jew (Ex. 30:11-16) was a form of poll tax. Poll taxes are administratively cheap because they are easy to compute and collect and difficult to cheat. Economists have considered poll taxes economically efficient because people are presumed to be in fixed supply. However, poll taxes are very unpopular because poorer people pay a higher proportion of their income than richer people. In addition, the supply of people is in fact not fixed over time: on average, couples will choose to have fewer children if a poll tax is imposed. The introduction of a poll tax in medieval England was the primary cause of the 1381 Peasants' Revolt. Scotland was the first to be used to test the new poll tax in 1989 with England and Wales in 1990. The change from a progressive local taxation based on property values to a single-rate form of taxation regardless of ability to pay (the Community Charge, but more popularly referred to as the Poll Tax), led to widespread refusal to pay and to incidents of civil unrest, known colloquially as the 'Poll Tax riots'.

Property Tax

A property tax is a tax put on property by reason of its ownership. Property tax can be defined as "generally, tax imposed by municipalities upon owners of property within their jurisdiction based on the value of such property." There are three species of property: land, improvements to land (immovable man-made things, e.g. buildings) and personal property (movable things). Real estate or realty is the combination of land and improvements to land.

Property taxes are usually charged on a recurrent basis (e.g., yearly). A common type of property tax is an annual charge on the ownership of real estate, where the tax base is the estimated value of the property. For a period of over 150 years from 1695 a window tax was levied in England, with the result that one can still see listed buildings with windows bricked up in order to save their owners money. A similar tax on hearths existed in France and elsewhere, with similar results. The two most common type of event driven property taxes are stamp duty, charged upon change of ownership, and inheritance tax, which is imposed in many countries on the estates of the deceased.

In contrast with a tax on real estate (land and buildings), a land value tax is levied only on the unimproved value of the land ("land" in this instance may mean either the economic term, i.e., all natural resources, or the natural resources associated with specific areas of the Earth's surface: "lots" or "land parcels"). Proponents of land value tax argue that it is economically justified, as it will not deter production, distort market mechanisms or otherwise create deadweight losses the way other taxes do.

When real estate is held by a higher government unit or some other entity not subject to taxation by the local government, the taxing authority may receive a payment in lieu of taxes to compensate it for some or all of the foregone tax revenue. In many jurisdictions (including many American states), there is a general tax levied periodically on residents who own personal property (personalty) within the jurisdiction. Vehicle and boat registration fees are subsets of this kind of tax. The tax is often designed with blanket coverage and large exceptions for things like food and clothing. Household goods are often exempt when kept or used within the household.

Any otherwise non-exempt object can lose its exemption if regularly kept outside the household. Thus, tax collectors often monitor newspaper articles for stories about wealthy people who have lent art to museums for public display, because the artworks have then become subject to personal property tax. If an artwork had to be sent to another state for some touch-ups, it may have become subject to personal property tax in *that* state as well.

Retirement Tax

Some countries with social security systems, which provide income to retired workers, fund those systems with specific dedicated taxes. These often differ from comprehensive income taxes in that they are levied only on specific sources of income, generally wages and salary (in which case they are called payroll taxes). A further difference is that the total amount of the taxes paid by or on behalf of a worker is typically considered in the calculation of the retirement benefits to which that worker is entitled. Examples of retirement taxes include the FICA tax, a payroll tax that is collected from employers and employees in the United States to fund the country's Social Security system; and the National Insurance Contributions (NICs) collected from employers and employees in the United Kingdom to fund the country's national insurance system. These taxes are sometimes regressive in their immediate effect. For example, in the United States, each worker, whatever his or her income, pays at the same rate up to a specified cap, but income over the cap is not taxed. A further regressive feature is that such taxes often exclude investment earnings and other forms of income that are more likely to be received by the wealthy. The regressive effect is somewhat offset, however, by the eventual benefit payments, which typically replace a higher percentage of a lower-paid worker's pre-retirement income.

Sales Tax

Sales taxes are levied when a commodity is sold to its final consumer. Retail organizations contend that such taxes discourage retail sales. The question of whether they are generally progressive or regressive is a subject of much current debate. People with higher incomes spend a lower proportion of them, so a flat-rate sales tax will tend to be regressive. It is therefore common to exempt food, utilities and other necessities from sales taxes, since poor people spend a higher proportion of their incomes on these commodities, so such exemptions would make the tax more progressive. This is the classic "You pay for what you spend" tax, as only those who spend money on non-exempt (i.e. luxury) items pay the tax. A small number of U.S. states rely entirely on sales taxes for state revenue, as those states do not levy a state income tax. Such states tend to have a moderate to large amount of tourism or inter-state travel that occurs within their borders, allowing the state to benefit from taxes from people the state would otherwise not tax.

In this way, the state is able to reduce the tax burden on its citizens. The U.S. states that do not levy a state income tax are Alaska, Tennessee, Florida, Nevada, South Dakota, Texas, Washington state, and Wyoming. Additionally, New Hampshire and Tennessee levy state income taxes only on dividends and interest income. Of the above states, only Alaska and New Hampshire do not levy a state sales tax. Additional information can be obtained at the Federation of Tax Administrators website.

In the United States, there is a growing movement for the replacement of all federal payroll and income taxes (both corporate and personal) with a national retail sales tax and monthly tax rebate to households of citizens and legal resident aliens. The tax proposal is named FairTax. In Canada, the federal sales tax is called the Goods and Services tax (GST) and now stands at 5%. The provinces of British Columbia, Saskatchewan, Manitoba, Ontario and Prince Edward Island also have a provincial sales tax [PST]. The provinces of Nova Scotia, New Brunswick, and Newfoundland & Labrador have harmonized their provincial sales taxes with the GST - Harmonized Sales Tax [HST], and thus is a full VAT. The province of Quebec collects the Quebec Sales Tax [QST] which is based on the GST with certain differences. Most businesses can claim back the GST, HST and QST they pay, and so effectively it is the final consumer who pays the tax.

Tariffs

An import or export tariff (also called customs duty or impost) is a charge for the movement of goods through a political border. Tariffs discourage trade, and they may be used by governments to protect domestic industries. A proportion of tariff revenues is often hypothecated to pay government to maintain a navy or border police. The classic ways of cheating a tariff are smuggling or declaring a false value of goods. Tax, tariff and trade rules in modern times are usually set together because of their common impact on industrial policy, investment policy, and agricultural policy. A trade bloc is a group of allied countries agreeing to minimize or eliminate tariffs against trade with each other, and possibly to impose protective tariffs on imports from outside the bloc. A customs union has a common external tariff, and, according to an agreed formula, the participating countries share the revenues from tariffs on goods entering the customs union.

Toll

A toll is a tax or fee charged to travel via a road, bridge, tunnel, canal, waterway or other transportation facilities. Historically tolls have been used to pay for public bridge, road and tunnel projects. They have also been used in privately constructed transport links. The toll is likely to be a fixed charge, possibly graduated for vehicle type, or for distance on long routes.

Shunpiking is the practice of finding another route to avoid payment of tolls. In some situations where tolls were increased or felt to be unreasonably high, informal shunpiking by individuals escalated into a form of boycott by regular users, with the goal of applying the financial stress of lost toll revenue to the authority determining the levy.

Transfer Tax

Historically, in many countries, a contract needed to have a stamp affixed to make it valid. The charge for the stamp was either a fixed amount or a percentage of the value of the transaction. In most countries the stamp has been abolished but stamp duty remains. Stamp duty is levied in the UK on the purchase of shares and securities, the issue of bearer instruments, and certain partnership transactions. Its modern derivatives, stamp duty reserve tax and stamp duty land tax, are respectively charged on transactions involving securities and land. Stamp duty has the effect of discouraging speculative purchases of assets by decreasing liquidity. In the United States transfer tax is often charged by the state or local government and (in the case of real property transfers) can be tied to the recording of the deed or other transfer documents.

Value Added Tax / Goods and Services Tax

A value added tax (VAT), also known as 'Goods and Services Tax' (G.S.T), Single Business Tax, or Turnover Tax in some countries, applies the equivalent of a sales tax to every operation that creates value. To give an example, sheet steel is imported by a machine manufacturer. That manufacturer will pay the VAT on the purchase price, remitting that amount to the government. The manufacturer will then transform the steel into a machine, selling the machine for a higher price to a wholesale distributor. The manufacturer will collect the VAT on the higher price, but will remit to the government only the excess related to the "value added" (the price over the cost of the sheet steel). The wholesale distributor will then continue the process, charging the retail distributor the VAT on the entire price to the retailer, but remitting only the amount related to the distribution mark-up to the government. The last VAT amount is paid by the eventual retail customer who cannot recover any of the previously paid VAT. For a VAT and sales tax of identical rates, the total tax paid is the same, but it is paid at differing points in the process.

VAT is usually administrated by requiring the company to complete a VAT return, giving details of VAT it has been charged (referred to as input tax) and VAT it has charged to others (referred to as output tax). The difference between output tax and input tax is payable to the Local Tax Authority. If input tax is greater than output tax the company can claim back money from the Local Tax Authority. VAT was historically used to counter evasion in a sales tax or excise. By collecting the tax at each production level, the theory is that the entire economy helps in the enforcement. However, forged invoices and similar evasion methods have demonstrated that there are always those who will attempt to evade taxation

Wealth (net worth) Tax

Some countries' governments will require declaration of the tax payers' balance sheet (assets and liabilities), and from that exact a tax on net worth (assets minus liabilities), as a percentage of the net worth, or a percentage of the net worth exceeding a certain level. The tax is in place for both "natural" and in some cases legal "persons".

Ethical Basis of Taxation

According to most political philosophies, taxes are justified as they fund activities that are necessary and beneficial to society. Additionally, progressive taxation can be used to reduce economic inequality in a society. According to this view, taxation in modern nation-states benefit the majority of the population and social development. A common presentation of this view, paraphrasing various statements by Oliver Wendell Holmes, Jr. is "Taxes are the price of civilization". It can also be argued that in a democracy, because the government is the party performing the act of imposing taxes, society as a whole decides how the tax system should be organized.

The American Revolution's "No taxation without representation" slogan implied this view. For traditional conservatives, the payment of taxation is justified as part of the general obligations of citizens to obey the law and support established institutions. The conservative position is encapsulated in perhaps the most famous adage of public finance, "An old tax is a good tax". Conservatives advocate the "fundamental conservative premise that no one should be excused from paying for government, lest they come to believe that government is costless to them with the certain consequence that they will demand more government 'services'".

Social democrats generally favor higher levels of taxation to fund public provision of a wide range of services such as universal health care and education, as well as the provision of a range of welfare benefits. As argued by Tony Crosland and others, the capacity to tax income from capital is a central element of the social democratic case for a mixed economy as against Marxist arguments for comprehensive public ownership of capital. Many libertarians recommend a minimal level of taxation in order to maximize the protection of liberty.

Compulsory taxation of individuals, such as income tax, is often justified on grounds including territorial sovereignty, and the social contract. Defenders of business taxation argue that it is an efficient method of taxing income that ultimately flows to individuals, or that separate taxation of business is justified on the grounds that commercial activity necessarily involves use of publicly established and maintained economic infrastructure, and that businesses are in effect charged for this use. Georgist economists argue that all of the economic rent collected from natural resources (land, mineral extraction, fishing quotas, etc.) is unearned income, and belongs to the community rather than any individual. They advocate a high tax (the "Single Tax") on land and other natural resources to return this unearned income to the state, but no other taxes.

Optimal Taxation Theory

Most governments need revenue which exceeds that which can be provided by non-distortionary taxes or through taxes which give a double dividend. Optimal taxation theory is the branch of economics that considers how taxes can be structured to give the least deadweight costs, or to give the best outcomes in terms of social welfare.

Ramsey problem deals with minimizing deadweight costs. Because deadweight costs are related to the elasticity of supply and demand for a good, it follows that putting the highest tax rates on the goods for which there is most inelastic supply and demand will result in the least overall deadweight costs.

Some economists sought to integrate optimal tax theory with the social welfare function, which is the economic expression of the idea that equality is valuable to a greater or lesser extent. If individuals experience diminishing returns from income, then the optimum distribution of income for society involves a progressive income tax. Mirrlees optimal income tax is a detailed theoretical model of the optimum progressive income tax along these lines.

Over the last years the validity of the theory of optimal taxation was discussed by many political economists. Canegrati (2007) demonstrated that if we move from the assumption that governments do not maximise the welfare of society but the probability of winning elections, the tax rates in equilibrium are lower for the most powerful groups of society, instead of being the lowest for the poorest as in the optimal theory of direct taxation developed by Atkinson and Joseph Stiglitz. See Canegrati's formulae

Views Opposed to Taxation

Because payment of tax is compulsory and enforced by the legal system, some political philosophies view taxation as theft (or as a violation of property rights), or tyranny, accusing the government of levying taxes via force and coercive means. Individualist anarchists, objectivists, anarcho-capitalists, and libertarians see taxation as government aggression. The view that democracy legitimizes taxation is rejected by those who argue that all forms of government, including laws chosen by democratic means, are fundamentally oppressive. According to Ludwig von Mises, "society as a whole" should not make such decisions, due to methodological individualism. Libertarian opponents of taxation claim that governmental protection, such as police and defense forces might be replaced by market alternatives such as private defense agencies, arbitration agencies or voluntary contributions. Walter E. Williams, professor of economics at George Mason University, stated "Government income redistribution programs produce the same result as theft. In fact, that's what a thief does; he redistributes income. The difference between government and thievery is mostly a matter of legality."

Discourse surrounding taxation generally places an emphasis on the intended benefits; healthcare, schools and so on, but rarely points to the harm caused by forced removal of possessions. Taxation has also been opposed by communists and socialists. Karl Marx assumed that taxation would be unnecessary after the advent of communism and looked forward to the "withering away of the state". In socialist economies such as that of China, taxation played a minor role, since most government income was derived from the ownership of enterprises, and it was argued by some that taxation was not necessary.

While the morality of taxation is sometimes questioned, most arguments about taxation revolve around the degree and method of taxation and associated government spending, not taxation itself.

If a tax is paid on outsourced services that is not also charged on services performed for oneself, then it may be cheaper to perform the services oneself than to pay someone else — even considering losses in economic efficiency.

For example, suppose jobs A and B are both valued at $1 on the market. And suppose that because of your unique abilities, you can do job A twice over (100% extra output) in the same effort as it would take you to do job B. But job B is the one that you need done right now. Under perfect division of labor, you would do job A and somebody else would do job B. Your unique abilities would always be rewarded.

In fact, Income taxation has the worst effect on division

of labor in the form of barter. Suppose that the person doing job B is actually interested in having job A done for him. Now suppose you could amazingly do job A four times over, selling half your work on the market for cash just to pay your tax bill. The other half of the work you do for somebody who does job B twice over but he has to sell off half to pay his tax bill. You're left with one unit of job B, but only if you were 400% as productive doing job A! In this case of 50% tax on barter income, anything less than 400% productivity will cause the division of labor to fail.

To conclude, depending on the situation a 50% tax rate can cause the division of labor to fail even where productivity gains of up to 300% would have resulted. Even a mere 30% tax rate can negate the advantage of a 100% productivity gain.

REFERENCES

Black's Law Dictionary, p. 1307 (5th ed. 1979).

Cobham, Alex (2007-01). "The tax consensus has failed!". The Oxford Council on Good Governance.

Corsi, Jerome, 2007. "The VAT: Menace to Free Trade", WorldNetDaily Exclusive Commentary, WorldNetDaily, February 3, 2007

Hoffman, Phillipe and Kathryn Norberg (1994), *Fiscal Crises, Liberty, and Representative Government, 1450-1789, p. 238.*

Johnsson, Richard. "Taxation and Domestic Free Trade". Ideas.repec.org.

Johnsson, Richard, 2004. "Taxation and Domestic Free Trade," Ratio Working Papers 40, The Ratio Institute, revised June 7, 2004.

Li, Jinyan (1991). *Taxation in the People's Republic of China*. New York: Praeger.

Olmert, Michael (1996). *Milton's Teeth and Ovid's Umbrella: Curiouser & Curiouser Adventures in History*, p.41. Simon & Schuster, New York. ISBN 0-684-80164-7.

Parkin, Michael (2006), *Principles of Microeconomics, p. 134.*

Ross, Michael, L. (2007-01-27). "Does Taxation Lead to Representation?". UCLA Department of Political Science.

Spencer Heath MacCallum (2007-09-12). "The Rule of Law Without the State,". Ludwig Von Mises Institute. http://www.mises.org/story/2701.

Steven H. Gifis, *Law Dictionary* (Barron's), p. 471 (2d ed. 1984).

"University of Chicago: Department of Economics". Economics.uchicago.edu. 2009-

Williams, Walter E. (2008-08-06). "Government theft, American-style". WorldNetDaily.

10

Deficit Budgeting

> "Besides the practical knowledge which defeat offers, there are important personality profits to be taken. Defeat strips away false value and makes you realize what you really want. It stops you from chasing butter flies and puts you to work digging gold."
>
> —*William Moulton Marston*

Basically, a budget deficit occurs when an entity spends more money than it takes in. The opposite of a budget deficit is a budget surplus. An accumulated governmental deficit over several years (or decades) is referred to as the government debt. Government debt is usually financed by borrowing, although if a government's debt is denominated in its own currency it can print new currency to pay debts. Monetizing debts, however, can cause rapid inflation (but does not necessarily do so) if done on a large scale. Governments can also sell assets to pay off debt. Most governments finance their debts by issuing long-term government bonds or shorter term notes and bills, often sold by auction.

As a common practice, Governments usually must pay interest on what they have borrowed. Governments reduce debt when their revenues exceed their current expenditures and interest costs. Otherwise, government debt increases, requiring the issue of new government bonds or other means of financing debt, such as asset sales.

According to Keynesian economic theories, running a fiscal deficit and increasing government debt can stimulate economic activity when a country's output (GDP) is below its potential output. When an economy is running near or at its potential level of output, fiscal deficits can cause inflation.

Primary Deficit, Total Deficit, and Debt

The government's deficit can be measured with or without including the interest it pays on its debt. The primary deficit is defined as the difference between current government spending and total current revenue from all types of taxes. The total deficit (which is often just called the 'deficit') is spending, plus interest payments on the debt, minus tax revenues.

Therefore, if $_t$ is a timeframe, G_t is government spending and T_t is tax revenue for the respective timeframe, then

$$\text{Primary deficit} = G_t \text{ “ } T_t$$

If $D_{t \text{“} 1}$ is last year's debt, and r is the interest rate, then

$$\text{Total deficit} = G_t + rD_{t \text{“} 1} \text{ “ } T_t$$

Finally, this year's debt can be calculated from last year's debt and this year's total deficit:

$$D_t = (1 + r)D_{t \text{“} 1} + G_t \text{ “ } T_t$$

Economic trends can influence the growth or shrinkage of fiscal deficits in several ways. Increased levels of economic activity generally lead to higher tax revenues, while government expenditures often increase during economic downturns because of higher outlays for social insurance programs such as unemployment benefits.

Changes in tax rates, tax enforcement policies, levels of social benefits, and other government policy decisions can also have major effects on public debt. For some countries, such as Norway, Russia, and members of the Organization of Petroleum Exporting Countries (OPEC), oil and gas receipts play a major role in public finances.

Inflation reduces the real value of accumulated debt. If investors anticipate future inflation, however, they will demand higher interest rates on government debt, making public borrowing more expensive.

Generally, a government deficit can be thought of as consisting of two elements, *structural* and *cyclical*. At the lowest point in the business cycle, there is a high level of unemployment. This means that tax revenues are low and expenditure (e.g. on social security) high. Conversely, at the peak of the cycle, unemployment is low, increasing tax revenue and decreasing social security spending.

The additional borrowing required at the low point of the cycle is the cyclical deficit. By definition, the cyclical deficit will be entirely repaid by a cyclical surplus at the peak of the cycle.

The structural deficit is the deficit that remains across the business cycle, because the general level of government spending is too high for prevailing tax levels. The observed total budget deficit is equal to the sum of the structural deficit with the cyclical deficit or surplus. Some economists have criticized the distinction between cyclical and structural deficits, contending that the business cycle is too difficult to measure to make cyclical analysis worthwhile. The fiscal gap, a measure proposed by economists Alan Auerbach and Lawrence Kotlikoff, measures the difference between government spending and revenues over the very long term, typically as a percentage of Gross Domestic Product.

The fiscal gap can be interpreted as the percentage increase in revenues or reduction of expenditures necessary to balance spending and revenues in the long run. For example, a fiscal gap of 5% could be eliminated by an immediate and permanent 5% increase in taxes or cut in spending or some combination of both. It includes not only the structural deficit at a given point in time, but also the difference between promised future government commitments, such as health and retirement spending, and planned future tax revenues. Since the elderly population is growing much faster than the young population in many countries, many economists argue that these countries have important fiscal gaps, beyond what can be seen from their deficits alone.

Before the invention of bonds, the deficit could only be financed with loans from private investors or other countries. A prominent example of this was the Rothschild dynasty in the late 18th and 19th century, though there were many earlier examples.

These loans became popular when private financiers had amassed enough capital to provide them, and when governments were no longer able to simply print money, with consequent inflation, to finance their spending. However, large long-term loans had a high element of risk for the lender and consequently gave high interest rates.

Governments later began to issue bonds that were payable to the bearer, rather than the original purchaser. This meant that someone who lent the state money could sell on the debt to someone else, reducing the risks involved and reducing the overall interest rates. Examples of this are British Consols and American Treasury bill bonds.

Ricardian Equivalence

The Ricardian equivalence hypothesis, named after the English political economist and Member of Parliament David Ricardo, states that because households anticipate that current public deficit will be paid through future taxes, those households will accumulate savings now to offset those future taxes. If households acted in this way, a government would not be able to use fiscal policy to stimulate the economy. The Ricardian equivalence result requires assumptions. These include households acting as if they were infinite-lived dynasties as well as assumptions of no uncertainty and no liquidity constraints. Also, for Ricardian equivalence to apply, the deficit spending would have to be permanent. In contrast, a one-time stimulus through deficit spending would suggest a lesser tax burden annually than the one-time deficit expenditure. Thus temporary deficit spending is still expansionary. Empirical evidence on Ricardian equivalence effects has been mixed.

Deficit Spending

According to the Keynesian economics school of thought (and related movements), Governments can attempt to stimulate the economy by intentionally running a deficit.

PRIMARY DEFICIT

Primary deficit is the pure deficit which is derived after deducting the interest payments component from the total deficit of any budget. In other words the total of primary deficit and interest payments makes the fiscal deficit. The opposite of a primary deficit is a primary surplus.

How this affects economic growth? (taking India as an instance)

> "Higher fiscal deficit in India has been one of the major reasons for higher level of inflation in the Indian economy as compared to other developing and developed nations. The cycle of high deficit and high inflation can be explained in two different ways. Firstly, high fiscal deficit indicates a high level of government borrowing that has a tendency to reduce the availability of capital. This leads to lower liquidity and consequently higher interest rates and higher inflation.

On the other hand, assuming that the government is borrowing to invest in the economy, this leads to increased spending that leads to greater money supply in the economy which can further lead to inflation if output fails to keep pace with this increased amount of spending (which has usually been the case in India). Further, to curb a rise in the level of inflation, the central bank resorts to a hike in interest rates. Thus, we see that high fiscal deficits could lead to higher interest rates and it could further fuel inflation in the economy if not checked adequately."

STRUCTURAL DEFICIT

Structural deficit forms part of the public sector deficit. Structural deficit differs from cyclical deficit in that it exists even when the economy is at its potential.

Structural deficit issues can only be addressed by explicit and direct government policies: reducing spending (including entitlements), increasing the tax base, and/or increasing tax rates. It can be described as more "chronic" or long-term in nature hence needing government action to remove it.

The opposite of a structural deficit is a structural surplus. Likewise, the opposite of a cyclical deficit is a cyclical surplus.

DEFICIT SPENDING

Deficit spending is the amount by which a government, private company, or individual's spending exceeds income over a particular period of time, also called simply "deficit," or "budget deficit," the opposite of budget surplus.

Government deficit spending is a central point of controversy in economics, as discussed below.

Government Deficits

When the outlay of a government (its purchases of goods and services, plus its transfers (grants) to individuals and corporations, in addition to its net interest payments) exceed its tax revenues, the government budget is said to be in deficit; government spending in excess of tax receipts is known as deficit spending. A deficit requires the government to borrow capital from the 'world market', increasing the level of (i) public debt, (ii) private sector net worth, (iii) debt service (interest payments) and (iv) interest rates. Deficit spending may, however, be consistent with public debt remaining stable as a proportion of GDP, depending on the level of GDP growth. The opposite of a budget deficit is a budget surplus; in this case, tax revenues exceed government purchases and transfer payments.

For the public sector to be in deficit implies that the private sector (domestic and foreign) is in surplus. An increase in public indebtedness must necessarily therefore correspond to an equal decrease in private sector net indebtedness. In other words, deficit spending permits the private sector to accumulate net worth. On average, through the economic cycle, most governments have traditionally tended to run budget deficits, as can be seen from the large debt balances accumulated by governments across the world.

Keynesian Effect

Following John Maynard Keynes, many economists recommend deficit spending to moderate or end a recession, especially a severe one. When the economy has high unemployment, an increase in government purchases creates a market for business output, creating income and encouraging increases in consumer spending, which creates further increases in the demand for business output. (This is the multiplier effect). This raises the real gross domestic product (GDP) and the employment of labour, and if all else is constant, lowers the unemployment rate. (The connection between demand for GDP and unemployment is called Okun's Law.)

Cutting personal taxes and/or raising transfer payments can have similar expansionary effects, though which method has a better stimulative economic effect is a matter of debate. There are no known examples of it working in the long term. The increased size of the market, due to government deficits, can further stimulate the economy by raising business profitability and spurring optimism, which encourages private fixed investment in factories, machines, and the like to rise. This accelerator effect stimulates demand further and encourages rising employment. Increase in government payroll has been shown to depress the economy in the long run.

Likewise, running a government surplus or reducing its deficit reduces consumer and business spending and raises unemployment. This can lower the inflation rate. Any use of the government deficit to steer the macro-economy is called fiscal policy. A deficit does not simply stimulate demand. If private investment is stimulated, that increases the ability of the economy to supply output in the long run. Also, if the government's deficit is spent on such things as infrastructure, basic research, public health, and education, that can also increase potential output in the long run. Finally, the high demand that a government deficit provides may actually allow greater growth of potential supply, following Verdoorn's Law.

There is, however, a danger that deficit spending may create inflation — or encourage existing inflation to persist. (In the United States, this is seen most clearly when Vietnam-war era deficits encouraged inflation.) This is especially true at low unemployment rates. But government deficits are not the only cause of inflation: it can arise due to such supply-side shocks as the "oil crises" of the 1970s and inflation left over from the past (inflationary expectations and the price/wage spiral). If equilibrium is located on the classical range of the supply graph, an increase in government spending will lead to inflation without affecting unemployment. There must also be enough money circulating in the system to allow inflation to persist—so that inflation depends on monetary policy.

A government deficit also has an impact on the economy through the loanable funds market. When there isn't enough tax money to cover outlays, the government must borrow. This increases the demand for loanable funds and thus (ignoring other changes) pushes up interest rates. Rising interest rates can "crowd out" (discourage) fixed private investment spending, canceling out some or even all of the demand stimulus arising from the deficit—and perhaps hurting long-term supply-side growth. But increased deficits also raise the amount of total income received, which raises the amount of saving done by individuals and corporations and thus the supply of loanable funds, lowering interest rates.

Thus, crowding out is a problem only when the economy is already close to full employment (say, at about 4% unemployment) and the scope for increasing income and saving is blocked by resource constraints (potential output). Despite a government debt that exceeded GDP in 1945, the U.S. saw the long prosperity of the 1950s and 1960s. The growth of the "supply side", it seems, was not hurt by the large deficits and debts.

A government deficit leads to increased government debt (often confusingly called the "national debt" or the "public debt"). In the U.S., the government borrows by selling bonds (T-bills, etc.) rather than getting loans from banks. The most important burden of this debt is the interest that must be paid to bond-holders, which restricts a government's ability to raise its outlays or cut taxes to attain other goals.

"Crowding Out"

Usually when economists use the term "crowding out" they are referring to the government spending using up financial and other resources that would otherwise be used by private enterprise. However, some commentators use "crowding out" to refer to government providing a service or good that would otherwise be a business opportunity for private industry.

Government Deficits: Good or Bad?

Whether government deficits are good or bad cannot be decided without examining the specifics. Just as with borrowing by individuals or businesses, it can be good or bad. If the government borrows (runs a deficit) to deal with a severe recession (or depression), to help self-defense, or spends on public investment (in infrastructure, education, basic research, or public health), the vast majority of economists would agree that the deficit is bearable, beneficial, and even necessary. If, on the other hand, the deficit finances wasteful expenditure or current consumption, most would recommend tax cuts to stimulate private investment, transfer cuts, and/or cuts in government purchases to balance the budget.

Unintentional Deficits

Not all national government deficits are intentional, a result of policy decisions. When an economy goes into a recession (say, due to monetary policy), deficits usually rise, at least in the U.S. and other large, rich, countries: with less economic activity, a relatively progressive tax system based on economic activity (income, expenditure, or transactions) implies that tax revenues automatically fall. Similarly, transfer payments such as unemployment insurance benefits and food stamp grants rise.

By contrast, other sources of tax revenue such as wealth taxes, notably property taxes, are not subject to recessions, though they are subject to asset price bubbles.

The reliance of California on state income tax, rather than property tax, due to property taxes being limited by Proposition 13, has been cited as an example of the dangers of an income tax-reliant tax system and a cause of the 2008–10 California budget crisis.

Automatic vs. Active Deficit Policies

Most economists favor the use of automatic stabilization over active or discretionary use of deficits to fight mild recessions (or surpluses to combat inflation). Active policy-making takes too long for politicians to institute and too long to affect the economy. Often, the medicine ends up affecting the economy only after its disease has been cured, leaving the economy with side-effects such as inflation. For example, President John F. Kennedy proposed tax cuts in response to the high unemployment of 1960, but these were instituted only in 1964 and impacted the economy only in 1965 or 1966 and the increased debt encouraged inflation, reinforcing the effect of Vietnam war deficit spending.

REFERENCES

Mitchell, Bill: Deficit spending 101 – Part 1, Part 2, Part 3; Neo-Chartalist (Modern Monetary Theory) perspective on deficit spending.

Michael Burda and Charles Wyplosz (1995), *European Macroeconomics*, 2nd ed., Ch. 3.5.1, p. 56. Oxford University Press.

Sullivan, arthur; Steven M. Sheffrin (2003). *Economics: Principles in action*. Upper Saddle River, New Jersey: Pearson Prentice Hall. pp. 403.

Vickrey, William (October 5th, 1996), *Fifteen Fatal Fallacies of Financial Fundamentalism: A Disquisition on Demand Side Economics*, http://www.columbia.edu/dlc/wp/econ/vickrey.html.

William J. Baumol, Alan S. Blinder (2005). *Economics: Principles and Policy*. Thomson South-Western.

Appendix

FINANCE MINISTER OF INDIA

The Finance Minister of India is a cabinet position in the Government of India and heads the Ministry of Finance. He drafts the general budget of the country, and is in charge of the national economy. Here in this list we have furnished the names of those who held this august office since first to the date

Finance Minister	*Term*	*Education*
Liaquat Ali Khan	1946-1947 (interim government)	Aligarh Muslim University; Exeter College, Oxford
R. K. Shanmukham Chetty	1947-1949	University of Madras
John Mathai	1949-1951	Madras Christian College
Chintamanrao Deshmukh	1951-1957	Jesus College, Cambridge
T. T. Krishnamachari	1957-1958	University of Madras
Jawaharlal Nehru	1958-1959	Trinity College, Cambridge; Middle Temple
Morarji Desai	1959-1964	University of Bombay
T. T. Krishnamachari	1964-1965	University of Madras
Sachindra Chaudhuri	1965-1967	University of Calcutta
Morarji Desai	1967-1970	University of Bombay
Indira Gandhi	1970-1971	Visva-Bharati University; University of Oxford
Yashwantrao Chavan	1971-1975	Pune University
C. Subramaniam	1975-1977	University of Madras
H M Patel	1977-1979	University of Bombay

Choudhary Charan Singh	1979-1980	Meerut University
Ramaswamy Venkataraman	1980-1982	University of Madras
Pranab Mukherjee	1982-1985	University of Calcutta
V.P. Singh	1985-1987	University of Allahabad; University of Pune
S.B. Chavan	1987-1989	University of Madras; Osmania University
Madhu Dandavate	1989-1990	Royal Institute of Science, University of Bombay
Yashwant Sinha	1990-1991	University of Patna
Manmohan Singh	1991-1996	Panjab University, Chandigarh; St John's College, Cambridge; Nuffield College, Oxford
P.Chidambaram	1996-1998	University of Madras; Harvard Business School
Yashwant Sinha	1998-2002	University of Patna
Jaswant Singh	2002-2004	National Defence Academy (India)
P.Chidambaram	May 2004 - Nov 2008	University of Madras; Harvard Business School
Manmohan Singh	Dec 2008 - Jan 2009	Panjab University, Chandi- St John's College, Cambridge; Nuffield College, Oxford
Pranab Mukherjee	Feb 2009 - present	University of Calcutta

Glossary

Accrued Expenses : Expenses that the business has incurred for which it has not received, or will not receive, an invoice, and that have not yet been paid.

Accumulated Depreciation: The total amount of depreciation expense recorded to date for the company's fixed assets. On the balance sheet, this value is subtracted from the gross value of Property, Plant and Equipment to derive a net figure.

Acquisition Cost: The amount actually paid to purchase an asset. This includes all costs associated with the purchase, such as installation, freight, and sales tax.

Asset: Anything that has future economic value. In addition to items such as cash and equipment, assets can include intangibles such as goodwill.

Bad Debt Expense: Losses for uncollectible accounts receivable.

Balance Sheet: A financial statement that lists the assets, liabilities, and equity of a company at a certain point in time.

Benefits: The total amount of indirect compensation that the business will provide to employees for each forecast year. Benefits are either statutory, such as payroll taxes and worker's compensation; or discretionary, such as health insurance, life insurance, and 401(K) plans.

Breakeven Analysis: An analysis tool that models how revenue, expenses, and profit vary with changes in sales volume. Breakeven analysis estimates the sales volume needed to cover fixed and variable expenses.

Budgeting: The process of determining and recording the expected financial results of a future period, generally the next fiscal year. In some organizations budgeting is limited to financial items that are shown on the income statement, while in others the budgeting process produces the three major statements (Income Statement, Balance Sheet, and Cash Flow Statement). After the target time period begins, the budgeting process frequently includes tracking actual financial figures against the forecast as well. There is considerable overlap between the activities of budgeting and forecasting. Budgeting usually involves a more detailed account structure and a finer time scale than forecasting, which typically covers between three and seven years of higher-level projections.

Cash Flow Statement: A financial report that expresses a company's performance in terms of cash generated and used.

Chart of Accounts: In an accounting system, the list of accounts to which transactions are posted.

Common-Sized: A term used to refer to a financial statement in which all items are expressed as percentages of another item in the statement. For example, a common-sized balance sheet might show all values as a percentage of total assets.

Common Stock Equivalents: Convertible preferred stock plus convertible bonds, stock options, and warrants.

Cost of Goods Sold: Another term for cost of sales.

Cost of Sales/Services (COS): All the costs associated with the goods or services that were sold during a specified accounting period, including materials, labor, and overhead.

Covenants: A set of conditions agreed to in a formal debt agreement and designed to protect the lender's interests. Covenants may include restrictions on debt/equity ratio, working capital, or dividend payments.

Current Ratio: Current assets divided by current liabilities. This ratio is a measure of a company's ability to meet its financial obligations in a timely manner.

Days Payable Outstanding (DPO): The number of days a business takes to pay its accounts payable, on average.

Days Sales Outstanding (DSO): The number of days a business takes to collect on its accounts receivable, on average.

Debt: A form of liability that represents money borrowed from banks or other institutions.

Debt to Equity Ratio: The ratio of total debt to owners' equity, used as a measure of leverage and ability to repay obligations.

Debt to Tangible Equity Ratio: The ratio of total debt to tangible equity, used as a measure of leverage and solvency. Typical values for this ratio vary from one industry to another. Lower values for the ratio represent a better financial condition.

Deferred Revenue: A liability that arises when a customer pays for goods or services before delivery is complete; for example, a one-year service contract billed in advance. Under accrual accounting, revenue must be booked when the obligation is fulfilled, not when cash is paid or received.

Direct Labor: Wages paid for activities directly related to production of units sold or services delivered, considered part of cost of sales. This does not include management and administrative salaries, which are treated as operating expenses or overhead. Also referred to simply as labor.

Economic Profit: A general term for various technical measures of profit in which adjustments are made to the traditional accounting definition of Net Income. Such adjustments are typically made in order to better estimate the future value of a business.

Equity: Also known as net worth or owners' equity. Equity is the net value of a company's total assets, less its total liabilities.

Expenditures: All purchases made by a business, whether in cash or on credit; not equivalent to expenses. Also known as costs.

Expenses: Resources used to support the ongoing operations of a business for a specified time period; not equivalent to expenditures or costs.

Finished Goods: Inventory ready for sale.

First In, First Out (FIFO): A method of inventory valuation whereby the goods first purchased or manufactured are considered the first ones sold. During periods of inflation, the FIFO method shows inflated profits compared to the last in, first out (LIFO) method.

Fiscal Year: The 12-month period, not necessarily coinciding with the calendar year, chosen to constitute a single year for external financial reporting and taxes.

Fiscal Year End: The last month of a company's fiscal year.

Fixed Assets: Another term for Property, Plant and Equipment.

Fixed Costs: Expenses that are assumed not to vary with sales volume within the expected range of sales volumes, such as rent or administrative costs. This is an important concept in breakeven analysis and in distinguishing between gross margin and contribution margin.

Forecast Year: Most people choose the forecast year to coincide with either the January-December calendar year or the fiscal year of the business, but this is not a requirement. Depending on the forecast start month, the first year of the forecast period may cover less than 12 months. In this case, assumption values that are entered for the first forecast year should represent the correct fraction of the 12-month totals.

Forecasting: Financial forecasting is the process of estimating future financial performance. The projected financial performance of a business is measured by using pro-forma financial statements as well as other indicators such as trend analysis, ratio analysis, and return on equity. Forecasting often takes a higher-level viewpoint than the related activity of budgeting. In broader terms, forecasting can also refer to estimates of broad economic activity in a country, industry, or financial area. For instance, analysts and economists release forecasts of where interest rates or stock market prices might go in the future.

GAAP: An acronym for Generally Accepted Accounting Principles. Accountants follow GAAP standards, conventions, and rules in recording and summarizing financial transactions, and in preparing financial statements. GAAP standards are issued by the American Institute of Certified Public Accountants.

Gross Margin: Net Sales less cost of sales (including both fixed and variable costs), often expressed as a percentage of sales. Also referred to as gross profit.

Gross Sales: The total of amounts received (sales for cash) and amounts expected (sales on credit) in return for products sold or services rendered during the given time period. Gross sales reflects sales at invoice values, before sales discounts and credit card fees.

Income Statement: A financial report that shows a company's performance over a specified period of time by subtracting expenses from revenue to obtain net income. Also known as a profit and loss statement (P&L) or an earnings report.

Interest Expense: Money paid by a business in exchange for the use of capital for a specified time period. On the income statement, "Interest Expense (Income)" is a single account that is the net amount of interest income and interest expense.

Interest Income: Money received by a business in exchange for the use of capital for a specified time period. On the income statement, "Interest Expense (Income)" is a single account that is the net amount of interest income and interest expense.

Investment: The expenditure of cash to create additional capital. Investment can be in income-producing vehicles such as stocks and bonds, or more risk-oriented ventures such as the purchase of another company.

Labor: Another term for direct labor.

Last In, First Out (LIFO): A method of inventory valuation whereby the goods most recently purchased or manufactured are considered the first ones sold. In periods of rising prices, the LIFO method shows a lower profit than the first in, first out (FIFO) method.

Lease: A long-term contract granting use of real estate, equipment or other fixed assets in exchange for payment. All leases entered in the Property, Plant and Equipment Detail are considered capital leases; operating leases should be entered as expenses in the Expenses Detail.

Leverage: The relationship between debt and equity. A company is considered highly leveraged if its levels of debt are high compared to its equity.

Liabilities: Obligations used to fund the operations of a business, including bank loans, accounts payable, and accrued expenses.

Line of Credit: The amount of short-term credit available to a business from banks.

Liquidity: A company's ability to generate cash in a timely manner in order to meet its obligations, often measured by the quick ratio or the current ratio.

Long-Term Asset: Any asset that has an economic life greater than one year. Liquid items such as cash are considered to be current or short-term assets.

Under accounting rules, intangible assets must always be classified as long-term assets, even if their remaining life is less than one year.

Long-Term Borrowing: Liabilities that represent money borrowed from banks or other lenders to fund the ongoing operations of a business and that will not come due within one year.

Management Goals: A set of conditions a business is striving to achieve. These may include requirements for debt/equity ratio, working capital, or dividend payments.

Market Value: The price at which an asset would pass from an informed and willing seller to an informed and willing buyer, assuming that goodwill played no role in the transaction.

Miscellaneous Non-Current Assets: An account for assets not including current assets, property, plant and equipment, intangibles, deposits, and loans made.

Miscellaneous Non-Current Liabilities: An account for non-current liabilities not including long-term debt (mortgage debt, lease debt, long-term borrowing, and shareholder loans) and deferred taxes.

Mortgage: A long-term debt instrument for the purchase of property by which the borrower uses the property itself for collateral.

Net Book Value: The acquisition cost of an asset less any accumulated depreciation.

Net Income: Total revenues minus total expenses, including taxes and depreciation, for a specified time. Also known as profit, net profit, or net earnings.

Net Income Before Taxes: Total revenues minus total expenses except the income tax expense, for a specified time. Also known as pretax income.

Net Operating Loss (NOL): The excess of business expenses over income in a given tax year.

Statement of Cash Flows: Another term for cash flow statement.

Taxes: Levies on the annual income of a business imposed by federal and state governments. On the income statement, this figure does not include property taxes, which are considered an operating expense.

Useful Life: An estimate of the period of time over which an asset will be of use to a company. Along with acquisition cost and salvage value, this measure is used to calculate the amount that the asset is depreciated each year.

Variable Costs: Expenditures that change in proportion to increases or decreases in sales or production volumes.

Variance: The difference between actual and targeted numbers for revenues, expenditures, or productivity. Variances are usually described as either favorable or unfavorable.

Working Capital: The net amount of current assets and current liabilities. This is equivalent to a company's liquid assets.

Bibliography

Cleveland, Frederick A.(1915)"Evolution of the Budget Idea in the United States". *The Annals of the American Academy of Political and Social Science*. 15-35.

Cobham, Alex (2007-01). "The tax consensus has failed!". The Oxford Council on Good Governance.

Columbia Encyclopedia, *Government*, Columbia University Press.

Corsi, Jerome, 2007. "The VAT: Menace to Free Trade", WorldNetDaily Exclusive Commentary, WorldNetDaily, February 3, 2007

Hedlund, Stefan (2004). "Foreign Debt". *Encyclopedia of Russian History (reprinted in Encyclopedia.com)*.

Hoffman, Phillipe and Kathryn Norberg (1994), *Fiscal Crises, Liberty, and Representative Government, 1450-1789, p. 238.*

James Macdonald, *A Free Nation Deep in Debt: The Financial Roots of Democracy* (Princeton: Princeton University Press, 2006). 564 pp.

Johnsson, Richard, 2004. "Taxation and Domestic Free Trade," Ratio Working Papers 40, The Ratio Institute, revised June 7, 2004.

Johnsson, Richard. "Taxation and Domestic Free Trade". Ideas.repec.org.

Joseph E. Stiglitz (2000). *Economics of the Public Sector*, 3rd ed. Norton.

Columbia Encyclopedia, *Government*, Columbia University Press.McCluskey, William J.; Franzsen, Riël C. D. (2005).

Olmert, Michael (1996). *Milton's Teeth and Ovid's Umbrella: Curiouser & Curiouser Adventures in History*, p.41. Simon & Schuster, New York. ISBN 0-684-80164-7.

R.A. Musgrave (1987). "public finance," *The New Palgrave: A Dictionary of Economics*, v. 3, pp. 1055–60.

Richard A. Musgrave and Peggy B. Musgrave (1973). *Public Finance in Theory and Practice*

Robert Barro and Vittorio Grilli (1994), *European Macroeconomics*, Ch. 15-16. Macmillan.

Robert Barro and Vittorio Grilli (1994), *European Macroeconomics*, Ch. 15-16. Macmillan.

Robert E. Wright, *One Nation Under Debt: Hamilton, Jefferson, and the History of What We Owe* (New York: McGraw Hill, 2008).

Ross, Michael, L. (2007-01-27). "Does Taxation Lead to Representation?". UCLA Department of Political Science.

Schick, Allen. (December 1966) *Public Administration Review* 26. 243-58.

Smith, Robert W. and Thomas D. Lynch. (2004) *Public Budgeting in America.* 5th Edition. Pearson;Upper Saddle River, New Jersery. 37.

Steven H. Gifis, *Law Dictionary* (Barron's), p. 471 (2d ed. 1984).

Walsh, Mary Williams. "Richard A. Musgrave, 96, Theoretician of Public Finance, Dies". January 20, 2007. New York Times: Business.

Willoughby, William F. (1918) "The Movement for Budgetary Reform in the States". *D. Appleton and Company for the Institute for Government Research.* 1-8.

Index

■■■